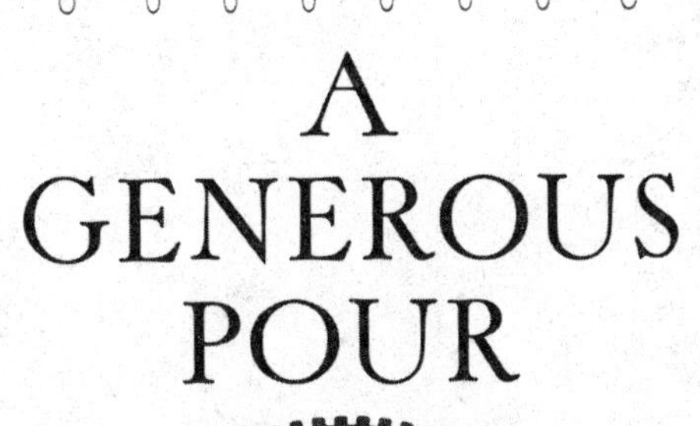

A GENEROUS POUR

TALL TALES *from* *The* BACKROOM *of* JIMMY KELLY'S STEAKHOUSE

by MIKE KELLY

A Generous Pour: Tales from the Backroom of Jimmy Kelly's Steakhouse

Published by Forefront Books.

Art Direction by Chuck Creasy, Chuck Creasy Creative
Cover Design by Josh Ford and Chuck Creasy
Jacket Design by Bruce Gore, Gore Studio, Inc.
Interior Design by Bill Kersey, KerseyGraphics

ISBN: 978-1-63763-113-3 print
ISBN: 979-1-63763-114-0 e-book

Library of Congress Control Number: 2022910858

DEDICATION

A Generous Pour is dedicated to the current generation of Kellys including those descendants not actively engaged in the restaurant business (such as my remarkable brothers, Tinker, Chris, and Bryan), who remain enthusiastic standard-bearers of our time-honored family tradition.

Regarding my phenomenal family, I must note that the singularly wisest decision of my life has been reflected in my choice to begin dating (and later marry) my roommate's best friend's roommate at the University of Tennessee. It goes without saying that my union with the low-key but indomitable and whip-smart Cathy Kelly, née Quillman, has blessed me beyond measure. We have raised two exceedingly independent, highly successful, and terrifically kind, generous humans: Megan and Bickham. In turn, we are immensely lucky to add two new additions to our family in our daughter-in-law, Carson, and our grandson, Grady.

In memory of my marvelous father, Bill, and my unparalleled Uncle Jimmy, as well as Johnny, Buster, Alan, Walter, Primus, Victor, Little Joe, and each of the Kelly team members (both then and now) who committed their hearts and souls to ensure that every experience at Jimmy Kelly's ranks as unforgettable, I raise my glass high, and say, as we Irish would, *Sláinte Mhaith* (to good health)!

TABLE OF CONTENTS

PART II
SMUGGLERS

PART III
SPEAKEASIES

PART IV
NASHVILLE'S OLDEST FINE DINING RESTAURANT

Prologue

A GREAT STEAK AND A GENEROUS POUR OF WHISKEY

Whenever I think things are tough in my life, I remember my grandfather and great-grandfather, John and James Kelly, respectively. Knowing the times they lived through, the difficulties they faced—from the Irish Potato Famine to the American Civil War, the Great Depression, two World Wars, and everything in between—I sometimes wonder if our present society could endure what they did. Maybe with all our specialization and technological progress, we've grown soft. So I think it's worth remembering what our ancestors endured and how their never-say-die spirit formed the country we live in today.

I didn't know James or John, but my grandmother Ethel was a lively storyteller. As a boy, I spent hours listening to her reminisce about the old days. It was fascinating. My uncle Jimmy and my father, Bill, also shared memories that absorbed me. So I began writing them down.

The stories in this book are true. Some minor details may be hazy, but I've done my utmost to present the facts as I believe they occurred. I've included a list of suggested reading at the end of the book, in case you want to know where I got some of my historical facts, or even if you just want to know more about specific events.

In his early teens, my great-grandfather James Michael Kelly fled Ireland during the Great Famine with a coil of copper tubing for a still and the knowledge his father had taught him about how to make great whiskey. After James lost an eye in the American Civil War, he earned his keep making Tennessee moonshine. He also sold ice to Nashville saloons and restaurants to chill the fish, game, and beef they served.

At age twenty-one my grandfather John Brady Kelly bought his first saloon, where he served fine whiskeys and wholesome bar food until Prohibition shut him down. To support his family, he took up the dangerous trade of transporting whiskey to Nashville from as far away as Canada and the Bahamas. In time, he opened an elegant speakeasy called the 216 Dinner Club, where he served excellent liquor and the thickest, juiciest steaks in Nashville. Celebrities, Grand Ole Opry stars, and famous politicians hung their hats at the 216 Club, and that's where John's son, my uncle Jimmy, earned his chops as a restaurateur.

"We make our guests feel like we're welcoming them into our home," my grandfather used to say. "We give them a great steak and a generous pour of whiskey, and they keep coming back over and over."

Jimmy Kelly's Steakhouse is Nashville's oldest fine restaurant, and it remains an institution in our city, a meeting place for all manner of personalities. When Uncle Jimmy retired, the restaurant passed to a new location under my father Bill Kelly's leadership, and now it's my turn at the helm.

I grew up in this business. My grandfather's 216 Club was still open when I was a boy, and I loved sliding down the banister of its grand spiral staircase. At Uncle Jimmy's place across town, my little brothers and I used to play hide-and-seek in the meat locker, running between the sides of beef hanging in rows from the ceiling of the cooler. I was tall enough to grab a meat hook and pull myself up off the floor so my brothers wouldn't see my feet.

Sometimes I'd watch the chefs take down the sides of beef when they were really "green." Many people don't realize that's when beef reaches its maximum flavor. I'd watch them sharpen their knives and strip the velvet green outside layer off the carcass. Aging makes even the finest meat more tender and flavorful. During this natural process, enzymes break down and tenderize the beef, giving it a unique flavor and ensuring utmost tenderness.

That's when I first learned how to handle a properly aged steak. In reality I continue to learn something new about the restaurant business every day.

Growing up, my brothers and I worked in the kitchen wrapping potatoes in foil, mixing cornbread, and making salads, and most often busing tables. I loved working with my dad. Like all the Kellys, he was a real character, a true restaurant man.

One Saturday night after a Vanderbilt football game, the restaurant was packed with guests lining the staircase waiting for a table, and an elderly lady sitting at a corner table waved for my attention. "Mr. Kelly," she said, "our dinner was wonderful and our waiter could not have been any better but . . . do you always let your busboy smoke a pipe?"

I looked around, and there was my father racing around the dining room busing and resetting tables as fast as anyone, with his hand-carved briar pipe clenched between his teeth. He had brought my mother for dinner, but when he saw how busy the restaurant was, he'd grabbed a bus tray and pitched in to help. I turned to the lady with a smile and said, "Not usually, but that's my father, and I learned a long time ago just to let him do whatever he wants."

The Kelly family history is colorful, to say the least, but one theme runs through it all: endurance. I'm writing this book not just to tell a family story, but to tell an American story, the history of tough, resourceful people who survived heartaches, wars, and the Great Depression—who lost everything, picked themselves up, and started over again.

PART I

STILLS AND SALOONS

Chapter 1

THE DAY MY GRANDFATHER MET AL CAPONE

Late one afternoon in 1925, John Kelly was walking down Chicago's Michigan Avenue, whistling a tune because he'd just had a grand day at the racetrack. For the past week, he'd been visiting Chicago's notorious speakeasies, trying to purchase bonded liquor for his customers in Nashville. As he strolled along, jingling the coins in his pockets, a black Packard slid to a halt at the curb, and two dark-suited men jumped out. Before John had time to react, they circled behind him and ordered him into their car.

These were the kind of men you didn't say *no* to. It was now five years into national Prohibition, and Chicago had become the murder capital of the country. With a thumping heart, John climbed into the back seat, whispering a silent Our Father and praying he might live to see his wife and children again.

As the car picked up speed, John struggled to control his fear. The men seated in front said nothing. All he could see were the backs of their necks. He knew they were strongmen, but for which group? The Genna Brothers, the North Side Gang, and the South

Side's Outfit were fighting to control the liquor that flowed from Canada through Detroit across the Great Lakes and into Chicago's central distribution hub. But John had made a point to avoid the rival groups. Why did they want him? Had he crossed someone's turf without knowing it?

They drove south down Michigan Avenue. When they stopped at the swanky Metropole Hotel, John was pretty sure he knew where he was. He'd read that this hotel was the headquarters of the legendary Al Capone. John had never seen the man, except in photos in the newspapers, but he'd heard about Capone's volatile temper. Capone's Outfit controlled two full floors at the Metropole, and several guards stood sentry in the lobby. As the two strongmen ushered John into the elevator, his nerves were twitching like electric wires.

They took him to the penthouse suite, and just before they opened the door, John straightened his tie and shot his French cuffs. Inside, a party was in full swing with piano music and noisy laughter. Burly men and beautiful women gyrated through the steps of the popular new dance called the Lindy Hop, and hotel waiters carried trays of highballs and champagne. Seated in their midst, on a broad leather divan, was the powerful boss himself, smoking a Cuban cigar.

Al Capone looked more like a dapper businessman than a criminal. He wore a dark pinstriped suit and a stylish polka-dot tie, and he appeared to be telling a story that made his listeners rock with laughter. When he noticed John hesitating in the doorway, a smile dimpled his chubby cheeks. He raced to the doorway to welcome his guest. "Come in, Mr. Kelly. I've heard a lot about you."

John felt more alarmed than ever, but he kept a calm exterior and took the seat Capone had indicated. A waiter brought drinks—Jack Daniel's whiskey for John and Templeton Rye for

Capone. Again, the boss smiled. "Sorry about the, uh, unusual invitation, Mr. Kelly. I hope the boys treated you OK."

"I'm fine," John managed to answer as he smiled back. Capone was not the man he'd expected. The boss was behaving like a gentleman welcoming a guest into his home.

Capone continued, "You're Irish, right? My wife's Irish too." He explained that his wife, Mae, was Irish Catholic, and they had a boy named Sonny. Then he asked about John's family. Clearly, he was trying to be sociable, but John remained on high alert, giving as few details about his family as possible.

Capone offered a Cuban cigar from a humidor, and while John lit up and puffed the fragrant tobacco, Capone said he'd always admired the Irish for their "smarts." John nodded politely, waiting for the axe to drop.

"We have a mutual friend," Capone said, raising his voice over the party noise. "George Remus in Cincinnati. George and I own a dog track together."

John's neck tightened. He'd been buying Remus's stockpiled bonded liquor for several years. Was that why Capone's men had grabbed him? As casually as his tight cheek muscle would allow, John said, "George has some trouble with the law, I hear."

Actually, George Remus had just been indicted on thousands of violations of the Volstead Act (the National Prohibition Act). That's why John was seeking a new supplier in Chicago.

Capone flicked ash from his cigar and scowled. "Don't worry about George. He'll shake off those feds."

The telephone rang, and Capone took the call. After listening for a minute, he grunted an answer and hung up. Then he turned back to John with a cagey smile. "I hear you've been buying a lot of liquor in Chicago, but no one seems to know where it's going. Tell me about your operation, John."

This set off sirens in John's brain. Was Capone planning to move into Nashville? John glanced at the strongmen guarding the door, then studied Capone's glittering eyes. Since he had little choice, he explained in simple terms that he'd been a saloonkeeper in Nashville before Prohibition, that his customers still wanted quality liquor, and that he was buying goods to fill their orders.

Capone opened his pudgy hands. "I'm just a businessman like you, John. We're both giving people what they want."

John took a sip of his drink, feigning an ease he didn't feel.

Finally Capone came to the point. "George Remus says you're aces. He says you've got a good head for business, and he's the man who would know. John, I want you to run my entire operation in the South."

John felt blood pounding in his ears. He held himself dead-still.

Capone continued, "This is your opportunity to go big, John. You'll be a millionaire, with full protection from my Outfit."

Now John's scalp was sweating. Work for Al Capone? Impossible. There were too many greedy hands reaching for too much money. He'd seen the criminal element all along the path where he'd found sources of bonded liquor—places such as Nassau, Detroit, and Chicago. He dealt in illegal liquor, sure, but John considered himself an honest man defying a bad law in order to provide a needed service for his loyal, longtime customers. He would have to turn the offer down. But would such a commanding person as Al Capone tolerate a refusal?

John flashed his warmest Irish smile. "I'm just a country boy, Mr. Capone. That's a generous offer, but I'm doing OK in Nashville. That's enough for me."

Capone's dark gaze bore into John like a drill. "You're sure about that?"

John forced himself to remain motionless, though every muscle in his body screamed for him to get up and run. He had to find a graceful way to appease this man, and he saw only one solution.

So he smiled again and said, "From now on, I'll buy all my whiskey from you."

Capone barked a short laugh. He must have realized this Nashville Irishman would not be moved by threats. Maybe John won his respect that night, and maybe Capone won John's as well. In any case, they came to a friendly agreement. John would buy Capone's liquor—at inflated prices—and in return, the Outfit would protect him. As the two men parted, Capone clapped John on the back and stuck an extra cigar in his pocket. "Remus warned me you were a straight arrow."

When John returned to his own hotel room, he noticed that, after exhibiting exhibiting such long, rigid control, his hands were shaking. Perhaps as he tossed and turned and turned throughout that sleepless night, he questioned why fate had brought him here. For an answer, he reminded himself that his father, James, had arrived in America carrying only one valuable possession, the tool of his future livelihood: a coil of copper tubing for a whiskey still. John was simply carrying on the family business.

Chapter 2

WHAT JAMES BROUGHT FROM THE OLD COUNTRY

My great-grandfather James Michael Kelly was born in 1833 in County Wicklow, Ireland, which is on the east coast facing England. Maybe that's appropriate, since England had so much to do with James Kelly's early years. By the time he was twelve, the Irish Potato Famine had begun.

Ireland's tenant farmers, such as the Kellys, were hard-bitten field hands, man and boy, woman and girl. Throughout the 1800s, they struggled from dawn to dusk on their small allotments, trying to supply the English market with grain. Their own main food was the potato: cheap, nutritious, and fairly easy to grow in Irish soil. By the time James was born, almost half the Irish population, especially the rural poor, depended on potatoes for survival.

In 1845, a strain of blight arrived via a cargo ship from North America. Because Ireland's weather was cool and wet that year, the blight spread like a black fog, rotting potato crops in the fields. The following years brought widespread crop failures, and soon the people of Ireland were starving. Rather than provide food aid, the English Parliament, which ruled over them, levied new taxes on Irish landowners to raise money for "public works relief," a euphemism for the workhouse, where the most destitute were put to hard labor.

Those conditions led to the Famine Rebellion of 1848, a failed uprising of young Irish miners, tradesmen, and tenant farmers who were protesting English rule. Their fight was quickly put down, however, by the pro-English constabulary.

Finally in the late 1840s, the Kelly family scraped together enough cash by selling the last of their valuables and bought passage to America for their three eldest children. Though the mother, father, and younger siblings would have to stay behind, their hopes rested on at least three Kellys surviving in the New World. His father charged James, the oldest, with caring for his little brother, William, and sister, Margaret.

As the family stood on the crowded docks of Queenstown (later called Cobh, and now best known as the *Titanic*'s last port of call in 1912) in County Cork, James's father, William, placed a coil of copper tubing in the boy's hands and told him to keep it safe. Even if James couldn't find a job right away, the anguished father assured him, as long as he found grain and good water, he could build a still and make whiskey to sell.

Then, like thousands of other Irish families, the Kellys parted forever. In that moment James became a man, in responsibility if not in years. Grimly, he led his frightened little sister and brother aboard the dilapidated, three-mast schooner, one of the many Irish refugee vessels that would later be known as "coffin ships."

Overcrowded, filthy, and in poor repair, the coffin ships were deployed by their owners for maximum profit. The passengers lived in squalid conditions, with only four feet of height between decks, and no sanitation. To keep costs down, the tiered bunks were plain wooden slats with a thin layer of straw, built six-by-six feet, to be shared by four people each. Maybe James noticed these alarming signs as he walked around the ship that first day, but he was too desperate to complain. He would soon discover there was worse to come.

In just a few days, it became clear that the ship carried too little drinking water and food for their overload of passengers. This was business as usual among the coffin ships. In one recorded case, the passengers were given no food at all during their forty-one-day voyage, and almost no water. As the weeks passed, James and his siblings slowly shared the cured beef and soda bread their mother had packed for them.

During the crossing, savage North Atlantic storms rocked the creaking old ship, terrifying and sickening young Margaret. Many passengers came down with dysentery from drinking the contaminated water, and all became malnourished. More dreadful was the typhus outbreak that spread quickly in the cramped conditions belowdecks. On some ships, the death rate reached 30 percent. On James's ship, one of the earliest to die was little Margaret.

In New York Harbor, James and William waited aboard their quarantined ship, exhausted, dehydrated, and probably in shock, as their arrivals were processed. Since both boys were illiterate, they signed their paperwork with an X. Then, at last, James met a stroke of good luck. He was hired "right off the boat" to work in bridge construction at a place he'd never heard of before—Nashville, Tennessee.

Since he couldn't take his young brother along, James reached out to the Catholic Church for help, and a kind priest arranged to settle little William with a local family. This was how Irish immigrants got by in those days. Their one reliable safety net was the Catholic Church.

After another family parting, James set out for the wild American interior, still a boy in stature but already a man at heart. For months, he laid the stone supports for a suspension bridge across the Cumberland River in Nashville. Only the second bridge ever built in the city, it was seven hundred feet long and high enough to allow steamboats to pass underneath. (It would be rebuilt more than once at the same site and eventually came to be known as the Woodland Street Bridge.) Every month, James sent back part of his wages for his brother's keep until William was old enough to fend for himself.

James made friends with his local coworkers, and when construction ended, he went south with some of them to the rich farmlands around Fayetteville, Tennessee, just a short hop from Lynchburg. When he saw the fields of tall green corn and the clear, spring-fed creeks, he knew he'd found an ideal setting for his whiskey still. And so, at age seventeen, James Kelly set up shop making whiskey.

Chapter 3

WHISKEY, WITS, AND WAR

The making of whiskey was lawful in the 1850s, but the US government charged a tax on liquor, a fact that James Kelly must have smiled at. Dozens of times back in Ireland, he had witnessed his father rushing to hide the family's small "poteen" still from the English excise men.

The Irish considered whiskey-making a natural right, but their English occupiers had passed a law in 1556 that limited its manufacture to "gentlemen, peers and freemen of the larger towns," and then only to those with a license purchased from the English Crown. Of course, Irishmen being Irishmen, they ignored the law and made as much as they liked. When the Crown imposed a whiskey tax, excise men began to comb the Irish hills, searching for hidden stills.

In Tennessee, the tax men were called "revenuers," but the dynamic was the same. The Irish and Scots immigrants who populated the Tennessee hills knew they could earn ten times more selling corn whiskey than they could selling plain corn, and they saw no reason to pay the government for the fruits of their own work. Like hundreds of others, James grew adept at making whiskey by moonlight.

After stirring his vat of corn mash till it reached the right consistency, he drew off the liquid and poured it into his "poteen," or pot still. This round copper vessel had a long swan neck that curved over to connect with the coiled copper tubing James had brought from Ireland. This coil was submerged in a barrel of cold water. Alcohol boils faster than water, so when James lit a fire under his pot, the alcohol vapor rose into the swan neck, then flowed through the water-cooled copper coil, where it condensed into a rich, white liquid that dripped from the end of the tube into a collection bucket.

Dipping his cup for a taste, James smiled. Corn yields more sugar than other grains, so his corn whiskey was smoother and sweeter than the barley whiskey his father used to make. Even without aging it, this was good stuff.

In time, James's whiskey drew a band of loyal customers, including a local Fayetteville boy named Felix Motlow. James and Felix were the same age and both loved the outdoors, so they became friends. James found the life of a moonshiner suited him well. But then came the day when shots were fired over a small harbor fortress in Charleston, South Carolina. James probably didn't understand all the reasons for the war we now call the Civil War. But when his pal Felix and other Fayetteville boys joined the Confederate Army, he did too.

In 1861, James Kelly enlisted with Turney's First Tennessee Infantry in the Frank Cheatham Bivouac. The following year, he took a glancing shot through the eye at the Battle of Gaines' Mill in Hanover County, Virginia. He lost that eye, and the other eye was damaged. And though he could no longer see to shoot, James stayed with his regiment, cooking meals, making whiskey with his portable poteen, and driving a camp wagon when the troops were on the move. The danger and hardship he shared with Felix Motlow strengthened their bond, but the misfortunes of war struck again when Felix was taken captive at Gettysburg.

The Civil War lasted four grueling years, and even after Lee surrendered to Grant at Appomattox Courthouse, some Confederates continued to fight. By the summer of 1865, though, the conflict was over for all, and seemingly by a miracle, both James and Felix survived.

After the war, Felix married a girl named Finetta Daniel, whose brother was a precocious young fellow named Jasper Newton "Jack" Daniel. The boy had left home when his father was killed in the war, and he apprenticed with a Lynchburg moonshiner, Dan Call, under the tutelage of an enslaved master distiller named Nearest Green. One year after the war, Jack Daniel started his own small distillery in Lynchburg, and for a while, he boarded with Felix and Finetta. James Kelly met Jack there when he visited his old war buddy Felix. But James needed to earn his keep, so once again, he tried his luck in Nashville.

Northern troops had occupied Nashville since early in the war, and while many Southern cities were decimated, Tennessee's state capital had thrived. There were plenty of jobs, and the refugees of war had flooded in, Northerners and Southerners alike, including freed slaves. The huge influx of young men accelerated the demand for strong spirits, and many moonshiners were drawn to the region.

People drank more beer and liquor in those days in large part because the water was unsafe to drink. Trash and sewage went straight into the rivers and streams, and the drinking water supply was neither chemically treated nor adequately filtered. The first reservoir to allow mud and debris to settle out of the water—the

8th Avenue Reservoir—wouldn't be built for another twenty-plus years.[1] So to avoid the frequent outbreaks of cholera and other sickness, people turned to alcohol.

Along with the hundreds of saloons in Nashville, there followed a stream of brothels and gambling halls, the primary male entertainment in those days before movies or other leisure options were commonly available. During the war, Union soldiers contracted so many venereal diseases that their Nashville commander loaded a steamboat full of prostitutes and sent them up the river to Cincinnati, only to have Cincinnati send them right back. As a last resort, Nashville became the first US city to legalize and regulate prostitution. All sex workers were required to get a clean medical certificate and a $5 license, or face jail time.

Nashville outlawed prostitution after the war, yet the world's "oldest business" didn't miss a beat. Hordes of young men remained in town to work, and the brothels and saloons still did a riotous business. The city's banks, lumber companies, depots, and warehouses were bulging with wealth and goods. The Louisville and Nashville Railroad was thundering with traffic, and the river port was busier than ever. Needless to say, the desire for good whiskey exploded.

When James Kelly arrived in Nashville with his poteen still, he saw that that the bridge he'd labored so long to build had been destroyed in the war. A new bridge was already under construction, though, and despite his partial blindness, James saw opportunities everywhere. Now in his early thirties, he was still hale and hardy. He found work driving a wagon, first for Shamrock Flour Mill, then for Northern Ice Company.

At night, he made moonshine. Hundreds of stills operated in the environs of Nashville to serve the growing demand. Nashville's thirst was so large that tons of corn had to be shipped in from other states. James's moonshine yielded a steady income.

With his years of practice, he could make whiskey blindfolded, which was just as well because the sight in his one remaining eye was weakening. Still, he was a tall, brawny Irishman with a gusto for life, and the eye patch only made him look more dashing. That same year, he met and married Ellen Byrne. Over the next few years, she bore him two sons, William and Edward. With the responsibility of a new family, James had to work harder than ever.

For the US as a whole, the late nineteenth century was so economically prosperous that Mark Twain and his coauthor Charles Dudley Warner later dubbed it America's "Gilded Age." Thousands of new inventions were patented—including the telegraph, telephone, and electric power—and the US saw the formation of vast transportation and communications networks. New rail lines allowed people, products, and farm produce to move freely. Agriculture, mining, and steel manufacture boomed. Many new banks arose as new captains of finance such as John D. Rockefeller, John Jacob Astor, J. P. Morgan, and Andrew Carnegie took charge of the economy.

In 1891, thirty years after James Kelly's war injury, he received a disability pension. Now fifty-eight and so visually impaired that he had to be led around by the hand, he could have simply retired.

Instead, he used the pension to start his own ice company, Kelly and Sons.

He and his boys made ice on a barge in the Cumberland River, then cut and stacked it in straw till the warm season. James drove his horse-drawn wagon around Nashville, selling ice to the scores of saloons, brothels, and restaurants that now filled his lively city.

Handling the blocks of ice was harsh, dangerous work involving numb hands, sharp instruments, and frigid temperatures. The huge blocks could slide easily, bruising and bloodying anyone who stood in the way. But James and his sons were tough.

Despite blindness and aging muscles, James did that work until the end of his life to support his large family. Altogether, he and Ellen raised five living children. After William and Edward came two girls, Mary and Nellie Clare. The youngest boy was my grandfather, John Brady Kelly.

Young John Kelly

Al Capone

CLOSED
FOR VIOLATION OF
NATIONAL
PROHIBITION ACT
BY ORDER OF
UNITED STATES
DISTRICT COURT
All persons are forbidden to enter premises without order
from the UNITED STATES MARSHAL

A federal agent is destroying illegal whiskey.

Gentlemens Quarter looking north on Cherry Street from Church Street

Advertising for the Southern Turf Club

The Climax Club

FIRST ARREST FOR VIOLATION OF MANDATE

Deputy Sheriffs Raid Saloon of Dawson & Burch on Cedar Street.

Pursuant to the latest mandate of Judge Neil, commanding that any person selling intoxicating liquors within Davidson county be arrested, Deputy Sheriffs Turbeville, Felts and Duke, acting under direct orders from Sheriff Charles Longhurst, raided Dawson & Burch's saloon at 11 o'clock Saturday night. This place is owned by Kelly Bros., but has been operating under the name of Dawson & Burch. John Kelly was arrested and carried to Squire Perry's office, where he was charged with running a disorderly house.

He was released on a bond of $1,000 for his appearance in 'Squire Perry's court at 9 o'clock Monday morning.

The raid came as the result of a tour of inspection made by Sheriff Longhurst and his corps of deputies Saturday. Visiting every saloon in Nashville, the officers paid something like a hundred calls in the course of the afternoon and evening, and at every place a strict inspection and observation was made. They were unable to find anything of a suspicious nature going on in any of the drink emporiums, with the exception of the one last visited, on Cedar street, and this they promptly raided and closed. No one except John Kelly was arrested in connection with the raid, but the doors of the saloon were barred against further admittance until this case is thrashed out in the courts.

When seen early Sunday morning Sheriff Longhurst made the following statement:

"In a message over the telephone this afternoon, Judge Neil reiterated his mandate of a day or so ago in regard to the arrest of anyone caught selling liquor in this county. We have visited nearly every saloon in Nashville today, going to more than a hundred places. In nearly every instance, it seems, spotters were at work, and as soon as our presence was discovered the lid was promptly clamped on tight. Soon as we went away the lid seemed to slip just a little.

"I intend to enforce the orders of Judge Neil to the letter. I made this clear and plain in a statement through the press several days ago. I have acted most fairly toward the saloon men, and if they do not appreciate it and continue to defy the law, they must take the consequences. We are here to enforce the laws, and we intend to do so as long as it remains under our charge. The judge has ordered that every person caught by the police and detectives for public drunkenness shall be indicted by the grand jury in addition to the proceedings in the city court. They will be compelled to tell where they got their booze or else accept a workhouse sentence."

Tennessean article detailing a raid on John Kelly's saloon.

The Tennessee State Capitol during the Union occupation of Nashville.

The Nashville reservoir the day after the wall collapsed.

Bill McCoy aboard the *Tomoka*

The *Tomoka* under sail

Gertrude "Cleo" Lythgoe, "The Bahama Queen,"was given the nickname *Cleo* because of her resemblance to Queen Cleopatra.

A skiff picking up a load of whiskey offshore.

Hams of illegal whiskey being stored below deck.

Cleo aboard the *Tomoka* preparing to sail north.

At Nassau dock loading whiskey

The origin of the word *bootlegger*

Lem Motlow leaving the courthouse in St. Louis

Lem Motlow

PROHIBITION ENDS AT LAST!

DECEMBER 5, 1933

Celebrating the end of Prohibition

216 Dinner Club sign looking south on 8th Avenue to Church Street

216 Dinner Club and Liquor Store

Swanky 216 Club Gets First Raid

Nashville's swankiest speakeasy, known to all those with a thirst as "216" because of its location, 216 Eighth avenue, north, was raided last night for the first time since it opened here, county officers announced.

John Kelly, proprietor, was arrested on a charge of possessing liquor and later released under $500 bond by 'Squire John Jenkins.

Seven or eight cases of assorted liquors were confiscated, but none of the customers in the elaborately equipped "club" were molested, according to Deputies Sheriff Lewis Hurt, Bill Corcoran and Leonard Castleman.

Newspaper blurb on the raid of the 216 Club

Chapter 4

KELLY AND SONS IN THE MEN'S QUARTER

In 1904, at the height of his success, James Kelly died. He'd lived seventy-one years and worked dawn to dark for most of them. But the company he founded lived on. Thanks to the continued surge of business activity in Nashville and the eating, drinking, gambling, and partying that went with it, Kelly and Sons Ice Company was flourishing. Indeed, James's sons were importing ice from up north to meet the rising demand.

Most of their customers were the bars and eateries located in the Men's Quarter, the elegant red-light district surrounding Printer's Alley in the heart of old Nashville. Home to fine hotels, restaurants, saloons, and bawdy music shows, the Men's Quarter was the place where lawyers and businessmen met to sign contracts and where state legislators did deals in smoky backrooms. Since the Quarter lay in the shadow of the State Capitol building, it was a hub of politics when the legislature was in session. Of course, no respectable lady ever ventured into the infamous Men's Quarter.

Through its center ran Cherry Street (now Fourth Avenue), where numerous publishers, including two major newspapers, operated their presses night and day, giving Printer's Alley its name. Beer and whiskey flowed around the clock. With the Bottled-in-Bond Act (1897) now in effect, the better saloons served *bonded liquor,* a term reserved for pure, unadulterated liquor of reliable quality, which was also the product of one distillation season. The good news for Kelly and Sons was that every chef and barkeep needed ice.

But winds of change were blowing through the Men's Quarter.

Since the early 1800s, women's groups had been urging reforms in civil society—first abolition, then women's suffrage and temperance. The temperance movement was originally founded by wives whose families were afflicted by the drunkenness of their menfolk. These women advocated limits on alcohol sales, but conservative clergymen soon demanded total prohibition.

One of the fieriest agitators in the women's temperance movement was a Kentucky radical named Carrie Nation, who was often seen in Nashville. After a brief disastrous marriage to an alcoholic, she came to believe that, like Joan of Arc, she'd been ordained by God to fight liquor. One of her tactics was to enter saloons with a hatchet, chopping at the bars and smashing the liquor bottles. In time, she gathered a posse of hymn-singing disciples, and she was arrested and fined dozens of times.

Tennessee legislators felt pressure from women such as Carrie Nation and from zealous preachers such as the Methodist revivalist Samuel Porter Jones. Over several decades, Tennessee had been gradually tightening its liquor laws, and the Adams Bill of 1903 had left only the state's nine largest cities still "wet."[2]

One indication of the changing scene was the story of a rowdy riverboat captain named Thomas Green Ryman. Captain

Ryman had been a regular at the Cherry Street bars until Samuel Porter Jones converted him to temperance. The charismatic Jones preached the evils of drinking in an open-air tent at the corner of Cherry and Broadway, and his theatrical style drew crowds by the thousands.

After Ryman's conversion, he thanked Jones by building him a hall to preach in, called the Union Gospel Tabernacle, just a block from the Cherry Street saloons. Ryman personally mailed three hundred letters to the downtown saloon owners, inviting them to visit a service at his new Tabernacle. Ryman died in the same year as James Kelly, 1904. After his death, his hall was renamed the Ryman Auditorium.

Large temperance crowds were still gathering to hear Jones preach in the years that followed. For the time being, though, Nashville was still wet, and the Men's Quarter was still hopping. There was still plenty of need for ice to chill the platters of fish, duck, turkey, venison, and beef served up each night. After James Kelly's funeral, the family held a conference. Their mother, Ellen, had been dead for nearly twenty years, so it was up to the grown children to decide how to carry on the family ice business.

After a short discussion, they determined that young John would manage Kelly and Sons. Although he was only twenty-one, he had the Irishman's gift for blarney, and all the customers liked him. Tall, muscular, and good-looking, John had thick black hair that curled over his forehead, and twinkling blue eyes. Like all the Kellys, he was known for honest dealings and a strong Catholic work ethic. What John had more than most was a savvy head for business.

William, the oldest, had a job with another company, but he would help out when he could. Ed was good with numbers, so he would run the office and keep the books. Mary and Nellie

Clare would continue to maintain the Kelly family household. Young John would be the "face" of Kelly and Sons, meeting and entertaining customers, making new sales, and keeping the business strong.

The minute their family meeting ended, John rushed across town to share the news with his sweetheart, the beautiful Hannah Feinstein. His prospects were bright, he assured her, and now at last, they could be married. A Catholic-Jewish union was not common in those days, but both families supported the young couple who were so obviously in love. Starry-eyed Hannah picked a date for their wedding.

Soon John became a fixture on Cherry Street, always with a winning smile and a good joke to share. He'd barely known his mother, who had died so young, and now he grieved for his father. But his new duties made him hopeful about the future. He had just unloaded a delivery of ice blocks at the back door of Mr. Edward A. Glennon's saloon when the older gentleman invited him inside to talk.

John rolled down his shirtsleeves, buttoned his cuffs, and followed Glennon into the saloon's cool, dark interior. He knew the Glennon family well because, like the Kellys, the Glennons were active members of Nashville's tight-knit Irish Catholic community. But Glennon was a rising executive at Royal Flour Mills, makers of Martha White self-rising flour, so it was rare to see him at his saloon in the middle of a weekday. John wondered what was up.

Glennon's saloon sat at the corner of Cedar Street and Cherry (now Charlotte and Fourth), and at that hour it was packed with downtown businessmen, railroad workers, streetcar conductors, tailors, bankers, and judges, all noisily crowded around the lunch buffet. Side by side, they plunked down their nickels for a pint of good German beer and one pass at the platters of fresh breads, meats, and relishes on the counter. Glennon took a seat in a quiet back corner, and John slid into a chair beside him.

For a while, Glennon spoke idly of the summer heat, the prospects of Teddy Roosevelt's presidential campaign, and the St. Louis World's Fair, where a Tennessee distiller named Jack Daniel had just won the Gold Medal for Best Whiskey. Obviously, Glennon was putting off the main subject, and John listened with growing curiosity.

Finally, Glennon got down to business. He wanted to sell John his saloon. It turned out he'd had his eye on John for some time. He liked the way the young man handled himself. He offered to finance the transaction, allowing John to pay him off in reasonable installments over time. He said the saloon would set John up for life.

At first, John felt more emotion than he could comfortably control. Gazing around at the busy crowd, he wondered if this offer were too good to be true. Sure enough, when he probed Glennon for more explanation, the older man admitted that some of his business associates had advised him to sell. With all the talk about temperance, it didn't look good for an executive in a family flour company to be keeping a saloon. Increasingly, liquor carried a social stigma, and Glennon had to think of his career.

John thanked the man heartily for the offer and said he would have to sleep on it. When he left Glennon's saloon that day, he drove back to the ice house without finishing his rounds. His mind was too full. The idea of taking on such a large debt and learning how to run a saloon, when he had just started managing his family ice business, was almost overwhelming. On top of that, he would be getting married in a couple of months, maybe starting a family. Could he do all that? More important, should he? Was it the chance of a lifetime—or a sucker's bet?

Chapter 5

JOHN KELLY BUYS A SALOON

John took the bet. A few weeks after Mr. Glennon offered to sell him the saloon, he signed the loan documents and was handed the keys. In almost no time, he found himself married to his beloved Hannah Feinstein and settled in the Kelly family home. Then he threw himself into the nuts and bolts of managing his saloon—as well as the Kelly and Sons ice business.

John hired a piano player to entertain customers, and he served all the finest spirits, including Nelson's Best whiskey from the nearby Green Brier Distillery, owned by wealthy Nashville businessman Charles Nelson. John also had kegs of rich, foamy German beer on tap. Anheuser-Busch was a juggernaut in those days, and the beer company supplied all the saloon's furniture and fixtures for free, even down to the glasses, as long as John remained their customer.

Every day, he and his barkeep polished the beautifully carved wooden bar with lemon oil and rubbed the brass chandeliers until they shined. He also purchased an enormous painting of a reclining nude woman to hang on the wall above the bar.

One afternoon, a diminutive man in a knee-length black frock coat made an entrance, sweeping off his wide-brimmed white planter's hat and calling a jovial greeting to some friends at the bar.

"Jack!" they responded. "How are ya, Captain Jack?"

The man's theatrical attire certainly drew notice, along with his thick black handlebar mustache and goatee. A group gathered around the little man as he made his way to the bar, and John took note of his diamond stickpin and ring. "Sir," the man said, "might you be Mr. Kelly, the new proprietor of this fine establishment?"

John had often heard about the illustrious Jasper "Jack" Daniel from his father's friend Felix Motlow. John also knew Felix's son, Lem, who was keeping books for his Uncle Jack and helping with operations. Lem was a bright, energetic fellow, and John was fond of him. But this was John's first face-to-face meeting with Lem's sprightly uncle, the maven of whiskey marketing himself, Jack Daniel.

Jack Daniel used hot air balloons and a cornet band to advertise his Old No. 7 whiskey. His chief areas of marketing had been in southern Tennessee and northern Alabama, but he'd set his sights on the rich profits to be made in Nashville. Recently the Gunter company on Lower Broadway had begun distributing Jack Daniel's whiskey in the city, and Jack himself was visiting all the saloons in the Men's Quarter to drum up business.

As I've heard the story told, Jack set up drinks for everyone in John's bar. This made him every patron's best friend, and his strong, smooth whiskey pleased every palate. The atmosphere in the bar soon grew loud and jovial with toasts and drinking songs. After that day, John featured Jack Daniel's Old No. 7 prominently on his shelves.

John's working hours grew long and late, yet the heady excitement of owning a place in the Men's Quarter made him feel like a king. He loved walking the busy sidewalks of Cherry Street, listening to the clip-clop of mule carts and horse-drawn surreys, while all around, Nashville's movers and shakers tipped their hats to one another as they met. John knew most of them by name from his years of delivering ice in the Quarter. Now here he was, walking among the grandees, sporting a linen suit and club tie and a sharp new dove-gray fedora.

His saloon stood just blocks from the famous Maxwell House Hotel and the beautiful Utopia Hotel, managed by William Polston, a man John greatly admired. The Utopia boasted the finest menu in Nashville, and its front bay windows were graced with magnums of wine and portions of venison, bear, seafood, and fowl from the chef's celebrated kitchen. Live sea turtles were chained to the lamppost out front, advertising fresh turtle soup.

Racehorse owners, jockeys, and city leaders gathered at the Utopia to eat, drink, and gamble. It was the sort of hotel US presidents stayed at—indeed, Theodore Roosevelt would visit in 1907. John himself sometimes dined at the Utopia with his wife, Hannah, and that's where his taste for fine food and wine first developed.

Farther along the street, a pair of sculpted angels hung above the door of the fabled Climax Saloon, built by liquor distributors George Dickel and Emmanuel Schwab. At the Climax, prominent citizens played dice, billiards, and poker, or visited the prostitutes in their third-floor boudoirs, or enjoyed the raucous cancan shows in the first-floor theater. Top stars such as Gilda Gray (who would become known as the "Shimmy Queen"), and the "I Don't Care" girl, Eva Tanguay, performed at the Climax during its years in business. John himself had attended one or two of those shows.

Local legend claimed that on a night former president Hayes visited the Climax, his strict pro-temperance first lady, "Lemonade Lucy," pushed through the crowd of men, stomped onto the cancan stage, and starting singing a hymn at the top of her voice to shame her wayward husband. That story always made John laugh.

And then there was the Southern Turf, the most opulent saloon on Cherry Street. Known throughout the South for its posh dêcor and upscale clientele, the Turf was founded by John's friend and occasional advisor, Ike Johnson. Thirty years John's senior, Ike had started as a young bartender at the Utopia before launching the Southern Turf. Ike knew the Men's Quarter inside and out, and John hoped one day to emulate Ike's success.

Between the ice company and the saloon, John's days flew by in a whirl of activity. A year after striking his deal with Mr. Glennon, John and Hannah moved into the apartment above the saloon so he could be closer to his work. Also, he and brother Ed hired more drivers, horses, and wagons to expand Kelly and Sons. Of course, John knew his investment was a gamble, but he moderated the risk by paying close attention to advice from Ike and the other saloonkeepers in the Quarter. Pure and simple, he cherished every minute, even though he saw clear signs that the Prohibition storm was still brewing.

Chapter 6

NASHVILLE'S DUELING FACTIONS

Each day, John diligently read two of Nashville's leading newspapers, the prohibitionist *Nashville Tennessean*, edited by former US senator Edward Ward Carmack, and the anti-prohibitionist *Nashville American*, published by Colonel Duncan Brown Cooper. (The afternoon *Nashville Banner* was a third newspaper.) A fine writer, Carmack railed mainly against his political opponents, most notably Colonel Cooper. Carmack despised Cooper for having backed Governor Malcolm Patterson, the man who vetoed the state's first attempt at a bone-dry law and who pardoned dozens of prohibition violators every month. It didn't help that Patterson had defeated Carmack in the governor's race.

In the summer of 1908, a bitter personal feud broke out when Carmack attacked Cooper in his newspaper for supporting the owners of a sleazy dance bar. Carmack wrote: "All honor to that noble spirit, Major [sic] Duncan Cooper, who wrought this happy union of congenial and confluxible spirits, separated by evil fates though born for each other."[3]

John enjoyed reading Carmack's florid language, but he couldn't have guessed what these acrimonious words would lead to. The elderly Colonel Cooper was furious. That evening at the Hotel Tulane, he told a friend that if Carmack put his name in the paper again, either "he or Senator Carmack must die."[4] The warning reached Carmack the next day, and all over Nashville, friends and relatives of both men conferred about how to intervene. Both men were deadly serious, and many leading citizens tried to calm them. But Carmack would not back down. The next day, he ran another sarcastic article about Cooper.

After that, both men armed themselves with pistols. Cooper's son, Robin, feared for his father's life and obtained a weapon to defend him. Robin tried to keep his father inside the Hotel Tulane that night, away from harm, but Colonel Cooper was enraged and refused to be manipulated. He insisted on walking out into the streets, where he would likely meet his enemy.

When the two men happened upon each other near the State Capitol building, Cooper ran toward Carmack, waving his arms and shouting insults. Carmack pulled his weapon and shot twice, wounding Robin. Then Robin returned fire and shot Carmack dead.

The effect on the Nashville community was profound. The idea of prominent citizens having a shoot-out in the streets was beyond belief. The Coopers were immediately arrested and vilified as assassins. In a packed courtroom, they were both convicted of second-degree murder and sentenced to twenty years in prison. When Governor Patterson pardoned his old friend Cooper, and when Cooper's son, Robin, was released after a second trial, the outraged only intensified.

Carmack had a large loyal following in the temperance community, and they immediately hailed him as a martyr for Prohibition. Silena Holman, president of the Women's Christian Temperance Union in Tennessee, declared, "the bullet that ended

Carmack's life will write Prohibition on the statute books of Tennessee."[5] Soon church leaders and Prohibition crusaders were using Carmack's murder to press for a statewide liquor ban.

The Kellys had always been active in local politics, but as John read the editorials and watched the news unfold, he saw clearly that the winds were turning against honest saloonkeepers such as himself. The following year, 1909, a draconian new Tennessee law prohibited the sale of liquor everywhere in the state, and a second law prohibited distilleries.

"Tennessee has been redeemed," wrote the prohibitionist *Nashville Tennessean*,[6] while an announcement in the anti-prohibition *Nashville American* encouraged people to stock their liquor cabinets quickly. The headline read, "Only a Few Days Before the Drouth!"

The news of this law shook the ground under John's feet. Would he lose his saloon? And what about the other establishments in the Quarter, all his best ice customers? Was his family's future evaporating before his eyes?

His friend Lem Motlow had taken over running Jack Daniel's distillery in Lynchburg two years previously due to his uncle's failing health, and he and John had many downcast talks about what Lem should do next. Indeed, Jack Daniel himself died in 1911 without knowing if his distillery would ever recover.

Luckily for John, the new law changed little for Nashville saloons because the customers ignored it and the police were induced to look the other way. As a token gesture, bars began to close on Sundays, but John's saloon trade actually picked up. One newspaper claimed that more liquor was being sold in Tennessee after the law was passed than before.

When the Utopia Hotel was raided, the police found a surprising number of state politicians inside "on official business." So many leading citizens were arrested that night, they couldn't all fit in the paddy wagons, and the Utopia's manager, William Polston, hospitably drove them to the station himself.

Then came the aftershock. In retaliation for the Quarter's lax attitude, Prohibitionists pressured the authorities to arrest Will Polston and sentence him to the workhouse. His arrest struck like a thunderbolt. Everyone in the Quarter was incensed, including John. People thought the world of Will Polston, and for good reason.

Every Christmas for years, Will had been shutting down his hotel to host an annual banquet for the needy. The waiters wore tuxedoes, and they set out the finest linens and silver to welcome Nashville's widows and children. The well-known social reformer Fannie Battle helped Will pass out the tickets. After a feast of turkey, duck, chicken, vegetables, and pie, each family would leave with a large basket of fruit, sandwiches, and candy for the holidays. Will Polston never turned away anyone who was hungry. In fact, Will had started Nashville's first bread line. And this was the man the Prohibitionists chose to punish.

As John well knew, the workhouse was a pit of hard labor, where inmates in striped suits literally broke rocks with sledgehammers. Dank, unheated, and rife with disease, it was a living hell. John worried about Will Polston, who was getting on in years and was no longer strong. When he was released after thirty days, John met him at the gate and saw at once that his health was broken. Indeed, in just two years, he would be dead.

Still, on that day Polston had cause to smile, because his time in the workhouse achieved one more act of kindness for his friends. The negative reaction to his arrest was so widespread that Nashvillians elected a new mayor that fall of 1909, a "wet" who campaigned on the promise *not* to enforce the state liquor ban within the city limits. That new mayor was the flamboyant Hilary Ewing Howse, and for a while, he changed everything.

Chapter 7

THE MAN IN THE TOP HAT

A newspaper reporter once asked Mayor Howse why he protected Nashville's saloons, and he shrugged it off. After all, he was a patron himself.

Like all saloonkeepers in Nashville, John Kelly supported Mayor Howse, for more reasons than simple self-interest. Hilary Ewing Howse was a man of the people, not a false populist but a shrewd benefactor of the working class. Many in Nashville's old-line business elite found Howse uncouth and possibly larcenous, and they allied themselves with Prohibitionists to oppose him. But Nashville's rank and file adored him.

Every street urchin knew Howse by sight. From his scarlet waistcoat to his shiny black top hat, Hilary Ewing Howse was a fabulous character. He owned a popular furniture company on Lower Broadway, and each week he rode around town on the back of his delivery wagon, waving and greeting one and all.

Before becoming Nashville's mayor, he'd won elections to the Davidson County Court and the Tennessee State Senate, thanks largely to his courtship of Black and poor white voters, a strategy that was very unorthodox in those days. Earlier administrations had implemented a poll tax to keep the poor and people of color from voting, but Howse shattered that scheme by using his own campaign funds to pay the poll tax for his supporters. Slowly and carefully, he was building a political machine to rival that of Edward Hull Crump in Memphis.

Once elected, he followed through on his campaign promises, building a library, a hospital, and a public park for the Black community. He also built a number of new schools, including Hume-Fogg, and he supplied food and heating coal to the poor. Also during his tenure, he was liberal in handing out jobs and favors.

When he ran for mayor again in 1911, he chose a Black man, Solomon P. Harris, to run with him, and Harris became the first African-American to serve on Nashville's city council since Reconstruction. That same year, a group of Nashville women's rights activists led by Anne Dallas Dudley met at the Hotel Tulane to form the Nashville Equal Suffrage League. It seemed that Howse's progressive leadership was opening many doors.

Most pertinent to John Kelly, Howse made good on his word to protect Nashville saloons from the state Prohibition law. Police raids became a joke under Howse, with fictitious names on the arrest sheets and ten-cent fines. In 1912, just before the *Titanic* sank, Nashville began once again to license liquor wholesalers in total defiance of the state law.

John Kelly and his friends were delighted, but the Prohibitionists and business elite were spitting mad. A group of Nashville power brokers dubbed themselves the Committee of One Hundred, and they made the mayor's expulsion a top priority. Yet Howse's popularity seemed to put him beyond their reach. Then, on the presidential election day of November 5, 1912, things took a bad turn for Mayor Howse—indeed, for much of Nashville.

Just after midnight, John and Hannah Kelly woke to a boom so loud, they thought a tornado had touched down. In reality, the city reservoir at the top of Kirkpatrick Hill had cracked open and spilled fifty million gallons of water into south Nashville.

The reservoir's granite walls were twenty-two feet thick at their base, and when the massive blocks split apart, no one in the city was left asleep. The flood snapped trees, toppled chicken coops, and swept homes off their foundations. Anyone looking out their windows that night would have seen an eight-foot wave charging down South Avenue, carrying off a family still clinging to their beds. Dozens of people went missing and were later found hugging the tops of trees. The flood caused massive damage (millions in today's dollars), but remarkably, no one died.

Early the next morning, John rode out on one of his stable horses to see the damage. He was shocked. The jagged crack in the wall measured 175 feet wide, and the once peaceful neighborhood to the south was a soggy, flattened mess. Residents wandered through the wreckage like lost souls, and muddy dogs moaned for their absent owners. People were still too stunned to begin the long cleanup. Everywhere John looked, he saw ruined lives.

In truth, the reservoir had been leaking almost from the day it was filled in 1889, but engineers insisted that the clay beneath its foundation would settle in time and seal tight. Unfortunately, they were wrong. The slow, steady leaks eroded the clay and undermined the heavy wall, causing it to sink and crack.

Since newspapers had been reporting the leaks for years, the business elite took this opportunity to accuse Mayor Howse of malfeasance. Soon after the flood, the Committee of One Hundred's leader, James Erwin Caldwell, telephoned Howse's office and demanded answers.

In late 1912, Caldwell was a powerful figure whose influence spanned far beyond the South. Since 1890, he had held the controlling interest in the Cumberland Telephone and Telegraph Company, whose lines crisscrossed the southern US and whose capitalization topped twenty million dollars (nearly half a billion in today's dollars). Earlier that same year, he had merged his company with Southern Bell Telephone Company, and he'd taken over as its president. He was also president and the major shareholder of the First and Fourth National Bank, headquartered in the Stahlman Building, one of Nashville's earliest skyscrapers. Added to that, he owned a large share of the Rodessa Oil and Land Company. Truly, he was a formidable enemy for the populist Mayor Howse.

As Caldwell stood in his lofty tower surrounded by his cronies, he barked into the horn of his telephone and scowled down at the modest City Hall on the square below. *Why hadn't the reservoir been properly maintained?* he shouted. *Where had the tax revenues gone?* Howse answered in his customary fashion, with friendly jokes and denials.

Caldwell and his colleagues responded by proposing a commission form of government, purportedly to make the city more efficient and less political. These maneuvers got them nowhere. In 1913, to their shock, Hilary Howse won his third mayoral term by a landslide.

But Caldwell and his friends were not deterred. Their next move was to accuse Howse's administration of graft. Once again, the colorful Mayor Howse simply laughed them off and continued his program of health care, education, and aid for the poor, constantly expanding the city's debt and continuously aggravating his opponents.

When he proposed a massive bond issue to cover the mushrooming debt, that pushed James Caldwell and his friends over the edge. Caldwell telephoned Howse again and furiously insisted on seeing the city's account ledgers. Nashville gossip had it that Howse answered, "You're welcome to see 'em. Come on down."

Yet when Caldwell's auditors arrived at City Hall, they found the city ledgers had mysteriously disappeared. Howse claimed to be as surprised as anyone, but many say Howse himself had tossed the books into the Cumberland River. No one knows for sure what happened. In any case, the ledgers were never found.

Almost at once, allegations of corruption flew thick and fast, and though Howse claimed complete innocence, the City Council held a judicial hearing to force him from office. Then, in 1915, the state legislature enacted the Ouster Bill, which called for the removal of any public official for unwillingness to enforce the law. The Ouster Bill was directed squarely at Mayor Crump in Memphis and Mayor Howse in Nashville for their refusals to enforce Prohibition.

Flamboyant as always, Howse demanded to be put on the witness stand, where he caused a minor sensation by declaring freely that he'd purchased liquor in Nashville. His words drew cheers from his followers, but he could not escape the scandal. Before long, he was out of office.

Meanwhile, in Europe, one of the largest and deadliest wars in history was raging. The Great War, which erupted in 1914, pitted all of Europe's great powers against one another, and when German U-boats sank the RMS *Lusitania*, killing 128 Americans, many cried out for the US to join the fight.

But John Kelly's family was fighting a battle of its own. His beloved Hannah had just returned from Memphis after nursing her dying sister through the final stages of tuberculosis. Tragically, Hannah had caught the infectious disease, and now she was struggling for her life. Hannah was not yet thirty, but the illness was stealing her bloom. Fever spotted her pale cheeks red and at times made her delirious. John sat beside her by the hour, holding her hand and praying.

The family doctor did his best, but all he could really do was prescribe cool baths for the fever and meat broths to strengthen her body. He couldn't save her. Neither could the priest and nuns who came to comfort the family, nor even Bishop Thomas Byrne, who prayed for them in the cathedral. When Hannah died, John felt bereft.

Eleven years was too short a time for a marriage. John tried to bear up, but he was reeling. Even though she'd given him three healthy children—Johnny, Jimmy, and Margaret—he felt alone. Everything he'd worked for, every success he'd known, had been sweeter because he'd shared it with Hannah. He'd expected to share his whole life with her, watching their family grow around them and welcoming old age together. Now that dream was gone.

His sisters, Mary and Nellie Clare, stepped in to care for his young children, and for the next few weeks, John went through the motions of daily life. He hired a young girl to cook and clean and look after his children, and he went to work each day, though his expression remained blank. Then came a morning when he remembered the Irish proverb his father used to quote: "A man of courage never loses it."

John lifted his head and realized his life had not ended. His children still needed his love and support, and Hannah would have expected him to endure. So once again, he threw himself into the task of expanding his saloon and ice company.

His task was not easy, though. The loss of Mayor Howse's protection caused a subtle retreat in the Men's Quarter. Most saloonkeepers, including John, quietly closed their front entrances, then reopened through their back doors while keeping a lower profile. For the time being, John's clientele became stealthy and cautious in their liquor purchases, and hundreds of Tennessee distilleries went out of business. Cherry Street's taverns emptied, and the demand for ice slumped. A veil of uncertainty reigned. But Nashville had not seen the end of Hilary Ewing Howse.

Chapter 8

ILL WINDS BLOWING

On a chilly winter day in late 1917, John Kelly walked along Cherry Street with his hat pulled low and a newspaper tucked under his arm. Ordinarily, the Men's Quarter would have been bustling at this hour, but instead, the area remained hushed and empty. A new fire-breathing prohibitionist had taken over City Hall—Mayor William Gupton—and he was determined to make Nashville dry. The bottles behind John's bar now held sarsaparilla and ginger beer, but they weren't selling. Many saloons had gone out of business, and John worried that his would be next.

Paradoxically, private citizens were still allowed to own liquor, and it was readily available in nearby Kentucky. But already, there was talk of a new statewide bone-dry law to criminalize both possession and transportation of liquor in Tennessee. Moreover, Prohibitionists in Washington were agitating daily for a national ban. John turned up his collar and gazed at the sculpted angels still guarding the Climax Saloon, now shuttered and vacant. Across the street, the majestic Utopia Hotel was gone too. After Will Polston died, the new owners changed its name to the Bismarck, and it was never the same. John frowned at its dusty windows.

A delivery truck rumbled by, an old Ford Model T retrofitted by its owner to carry coal. John waved at the driver, glad to see that, at least somewhere in the Quarter, a fire still burned.

The headlines in his newspaper were all about the "War to End All Wars," which had deteriorated into a savage battle of attrition along Europe's Western Front. That meandering no-man's-land of barbed wire, foxholes, and fortified trenches extended now from the North Sea to France, where two of the war's most vicious battles had been fought the previous year—Verdun and the Somme. Many in Congress were urging President Woodrow Wilson to enter the war. Yet others still held to an isolationist view, remembering George Washington's warning against the "perils of foreign entanglements" in his Farewell Address.

John Kelly read of their debates with concern. Anti-German fervor ran high, and John had noticed more than one of his German friends acting skittish at public gatherings. He thought the war sloganeers were being unfair to Nashville's large German community. He himself felt divided about entering the war. At thirty-four, he still had youthful good looks and broad shoulders, and, though his hair had turned prematurely silver, he was not too old to fight. Great Britain was already conscripting men for its army. If the US entered the war and called him up, would he go?

Of course, he worried about his children. His sons, Johnny and Jimmy, were such a pair of cutups; they constantly amused him. And his little daughter, Margaret, was the light of his heart. He didn't want to leave them. But there was more in the news to make him think twice about entering the war.

Earlier that year, he'd read that a schoolmaster named Patrick Pearse had led a few hundred citizens to fight throughout the streets of Dublin for Irish independence. They'd occupied several buildings, and all through Easter Holy Week they'd held their ground, until thousands of British troops subdued them with artillery. Their rebellion was called the Easter Rising, and it marked the beginning of the end of Ireland's long struggle for freedom from British rule.

John honored those courageous Irishmen, and he wasn't sure he could stand with the British now. His father, James, had always hated the British for the way they'd treated his family back in Ireland.

As John walked along Cherry Street muffled in his overcoat, he gazed at the empty sidewalks with a sense of uneasiness. Abruptly, he came to a halt at the entrance of the former Southern Turf saloon, once the jewel of Cherry Street. Now this beautiful building was being turned into office space. John ran a hand across his mouth, remembering the Turf's owner, Ike Johnson. Ike had offered friendship and wise advice to him, and John missed him sorely.

Few people beyond Ike's close circle knew how generous he had been to friends and strangers alike, how many Nashville charities he'd supported, or families he'd aided, or businesses he'd saved with a timely personal loan. Ike even made sure every newspaper boy in the Quarter had a decent pair of shoes, but he'd shied away from public recognition. Truly, he'd been a tenderhearted man.

John peered up at the third-floor apartment. It was where Ike had lived for twenty years until his building had been taken over by the *Tennessean*, the very Prohibitionist newspaper that had championed closing his saloon. Right there in that apartment on March 19, 1916, Ike Johnson had put a bullet through his brain.

The *Tennessean* ran an article soon after, stating that Ike had called its editor the day before his death to say, "You may have occasion to say something more of the building and of me, but don't throw any bouquets at me."[7]

This was typical of Ike Johnson's modesty. Yet despite the publication's long-term opposition to saloons such as the Southern Turf, their article went on to reveal exactly the kind of life Ike Johnson had lived.

The editor wrote, "There are thousands of people in Nashville who have been helped in one way or another by this man in the line of what is ordinarily called charity. He constantly had men looking for people in need, and he supplied their needs without ever letting any one of them know whence the supplies came. But his charity went far beyond that. There are a number of men now prominent and influential in business and professional life in Nashville whom Mr. Johnson helped over difficulties that, without help, would have meant their permanent ruin. He was a close observer, and seemed possessed of a sort of intuition as to when a man was in straits, financial or otherwise. . . . In the flow of his generosity, he knew no class or creed or race. In short, it is doubtful if another man ever lived in Nashville whose spirit of helpfulness was so free and all-embracing."[8]

John Kelly lowered his head and walked on. He was not normally one to brood, but the suicide of his friend had hit hard. Still, as desolate as he felt, he knew Ike's choice was not the right answer. Like all the Kellys, John was a devout Catholic who considered suicide a mortal sin. Besides, he could never abandon his family. It was for their benefit that he'd worked so long to build his business. Nevertheless, here he was, a recent widower with three young children to raise, and his income was plummeting. If things went on at this rate, he would soon be ruined.

He buttoned his overcoat and marched on. There was no sense in whining over what was lost. For his children's sake, he had to figure out something new. "A man of courage never loses it," he said to himself repeatedly.

So far, he had not closed his saloon. Its elaborately carved wooden bar still gleamed with lemon oil, and the brass chandeliers still shone from frequent polishing. The enormous painting of the naked woman still smiled at all who entered, but John's stock of fine spirits was packed away in the attic. For the moment, it was still legal to own stock that had been already purchased, but he couldn't sell it. He hoped, at least, that he could barter some whiskey to his ice company employees in exchange for reduced wages because Kelly and Sons Ice Company was failing too.

The shuttered restaurants and taverns of the Men's Quarter had been the core of his ice business. His residential customers didn't order enough ice to pick up the slack. If he didn't find new ice customers soon, the entire family business could collapse.

Brooding about the ice situation sent him off on a new tangent. A few weeks earlier, a young friend had telephoned him, desperate to buy liquor for a dinner party. The young man had just been made partner in a law firm, and he was hosting his new colleagues in his home that evening. But the whiskey he'd procured from a bootlegger—supposedly bonded, but he doubted it—tasted more like paint thinner than bourbon. He was in a tight spot. Would John slip four bottles in with his ice delivery that day?

John knew the law firm's sophisticated partners. They'd all been regulars at his saloon, so he understood the young man's predicament. Of course he agreed to help. In gratitude the young lawyer insisted on paying John the same high price he'd paid for the undrinkable stuff.

After that, one thing led to another, and the firm's other partners asked John to add a few bottles to their ice orders. Naturally, he felt obliged to accommodate his long-time customers, and now word was spreading. Almost every day, he got a new request. The inventory in his attic would soon run out. But what if . . .

As his leather shoes pounded the pavement, the gears of his quick mind turned. The Prohibitionists might put an end to saloons, but they couldn't arrest Nashville's appetite for quality whiskey. The law they'd passed was ill-conceived. Half the people of Nashville said so.

All at once, an idea ripened and bloomed in John's mind. Delivering liquor with the ice was a natural fit, and he could find plenty of bonded whiskey in Kentucky. Bringing it back to Nashville might be a bit risky, yes, but John wasn't intimidated by the idea of risk. His plan seemed ideal. He could oblige his customers, support his family, and keep the ice company afloat. The question was, was it right?

He faced west, shading his eyes from the afternoon sun. From where he stood, he could almost see the spires of Vanderbilt University rising along West End Avenue. He could vividly picture the bell tower of his family's church, the gleaming new Cathedral of the Incarnation.

That's what I'll do, John told himself. *I'll go there to pray for guidance.*

Chapter 9

THE BISHOP'S ADVICE

John Kelly thought nothing of walking the two miles from the Men's Quarter to the new Cathedral of the Incarnation. He made that particular hike often, and the exercise it provided usually improved his mood. As he made his way up Broadway, electric streetcars glided past him, en route to the magnificent Union Station with its castellated towers and modern mechanical clock.

After passing the station, John crossed the viaduct that spanned Nashville's teeming railroad yard in the gulch below. Eight train lines intersected here. Whenever John stood on the bridge watching the throngs of passengers and the puffing steam locomotives, he felt the city's energy pulsing through his veins. Even now that the city fathers wanted to close his operation down, he still felt proud to be a part of this booming city.

He hurried on across the viaduct, then climbed the rise to the West End and sighted the cathedral a few blocks away. Its yellow glazed brick and red tile roof glowed like a beacon of hope in the afternoon sun.

As John stepped from afternoon sunlight into the vestibule's cool dimness, he removed his hat and waited for his eyes adjust. Inside the cathedral's nave, all was quiet and still; the scent of a familiar candle wax hung in the air. Soft light filtered down from the high clerestory windows, casting tiny rainbows on the pews below; the white marble crucifix behind the sanctuary seemed to beckon John forward.

Hat in hand, he dipped his fingertips in the font of holy water and made the sign of the cross. Then he proceeded down the aisle, peering at the stations of the cross depicted in scagliola plasterwork along the east and west walls. The fourteen scenes of Jesus bearing and suffering on the cross made him thoughtful. Near the apse, he approached a side altar, as he always did, to light a votive candle for his dear Hannah. Then, after dropping a coin in the offering box, he found his way to a pew, knelt down, and closed his eyes.

As was his custom, he laced his fingers together and prayed in silence, picturing his brown-eyed Hannah and the three children she'd given him, the three innocent souls he felt honor-bound to protect. Again, he struggled over the decision he had to make. He prayed not with words but with hope for guidance.

When he opened his eyes, he became aware of a presence close beside him in the pew. He turned, and to his surprise, there sat Bishop Thomas Sebastian Byrne, the fifth bishop of Nashville. Still a vigorous man in his mid-seventies, Bishop Byrne had thinning gray hair, but his eyebrows remained as thick and black as ever. He wore a simple black cassock and skullcap, and he seemed to look directly into John's heart.

When Bishop Byrne had first moved to Nashville, John had been only a boy, and he'd grown up listening to the bishop's homilies. The Church had played a steadfast role in the Kelly family's life, and John's father, James, had been an active Catholic. For years, James Kelly had organized the St. Patrick's Day celebration, a large and popular event in Nashville. And every Christmas, James would deliver a gift of his sweet corn whiskey to the bishop's door. After James's death, John continued the tradition with a case or two of Jack Daniel's. The bishop had always welcomed the gift with a hearty laugh and an invitation to share a glass.

John marveled at Bishop Byrne's tireless energy. He was known throughout Nashville as the man who had built the Cathedral of the Incarnation.[9] He'd earned much of the money by his own hand, translating five volumes of Italian sermons written by the Bishop of Cremona. He'd also translated French religious works, and all his books sold well. He'd built the rectory and school first so he could be on hand night and day during the construction of the majestic cathedral. After years of effort, he had finally opened its doors just three years earlier, in 1914.

Since coming to Nashville, not only had Bishop Byrne raised enough money to pay off the diocese debts, he had also launched many benevolent organizations and added new parishes. He'd opened Nashville's first Catholic school for African-Americans, and he'd worked to establish Nashville's parishes on geographical lines rather than ethnic ones. Until the early 1900s, a diocese would have its "Irish church," its "Italian church," its "German church," and so on, but Bishop Byrne believed this kept the faithful apart and limited the growth of Catholicism. For years, Nashville's Catholic leaders argued over the issue, but in the end, the bishop's view prevailed.

Though John admired Bishop Byrne's many accomplishments, what counted more was that John loved him as a friend. Through years of talks by the rectory hearth, John had learned the bishop's story. Orphaned as an infant, Thomas Byrne grew up in poverty, and he'd earned his keep from age eleven by working as a factory machinist. This put him behind in school, but he was determined to become a priest. After much effort, luck, and help from friends, he was able to pursue his dream at the North American College in Rome. Regrettably, the damp winters made him ill, and his time in Rome was cut short. Still he persevered in his studies and became a scholar of the Church, a gifted writer and translator whose intelligence was respected by all.

John knew the bishop had experienced hardship firsthand. He knew Thomas Byrne understood personal loss and the need to endure. So when the bishop asked if John's heart was troubled, John felt free to open up and speak his thoughts without reserve.

They talked about his wife at first, and John confessed that he still missed her. Then he explained his situation in detail, the political atmosphere and the anti-liquor laws that were strangling his business. The saloon and the ice company were losing too much money, and soon he would have to close down. He spoke of his lost income and his anxiety for his children's future. Through it all, the bishop listened and nodded quietly.

Then John described how his former saloon customers hadn't disappeared just because of a law. They still wanted good whiskey—not the watered-down, adulterated stuff, but the real thing. Many friends had called, seeking his help, and he told the bishop how he might continue serving them as he always had before, delivering fine bonded liquor they could trust and enjoy. *Uisce beatha*, the bishop told him, explaining that the Irish Gaelic words translated as "the water of life."

John admired the bishop's learning. For a while, they discussed the vagaries of illegal liquor, too often diluted or flavored with artificial ingredients. Some unscrupulous bootleggers even sold deadly wood alcohol made from distilling wood. Blindness and deaths were already being reported due to that. John abhorred these practices, but if Tennessee's prohibition continued, he knew they would only get worse.

Another option was moonshine, such as the sour mash liquor his father used to make by moonlight. But lately, the moonshine trade's rising profits were drawing ruthless men of little skill. Some even used auto radiators as condensers in their stills, leeching poisonous antifreeze and lead into the liquor.

John said his aim was to provide his customers with name-brand whiskey bottled by the best distillers. Liquor was still legal in Kentucky, and he'd made many friends there. He traveled to Louisville often for the horse races so his trips would not raise suspicion. His own father had flouted liquor laws, as had James's father before him in Ireland. John turned to the bishop and asked, *Should an honest man break a bad law? Was it right or wrong?*

Bishop Byrne raised his eyes to the cathedral's sculpted ceiling as if deep in thought. After several moments, he spoke softly, reminding John of the many challenges his father, James, had faced, and how he'd always put his family first and labored to provide for them. Family was a man's most important earthly obligation.

Next, he noted the Catholic view that alcohol was a gift from God, as described in the Bible, and that Christ himself had consecrated wine at the Last Supper. Christians had been consuming alcohol as part of normal life for centuries, and only recently had the evangelicals begun to speak of it as a sin. Now they were making abstinence the law of the land, imposing their religious beliefs on all. Needless to say, the Catholic Church had a long history of resistance to unjust law.

The bishop urged John to think carefully and always to act with integrity and compassion, whatever path he took. His final advice was, "You must do what is necessary to support your family." Then they prayed together, with much emotion.

After the prayer, John felt relieved and lightened. As he was turning to leave, the bishop casually asked how he planned to sell his whiskey in Nashville without getting caught. John's blue eyes twinkled, and he flashed his merriest smile. That, he said, was the easy part. Kelly and Sons wagons would deliver liquor to people's homes hidden in their weekly order of ice.

Chapter 10

ROADS, RACETRACKS, AND RAILWAYS

The term *bootlegging* came into use in the late 1800s, when many states besides Tennessee began to tighten their liquor laws in deference to the temperance movement. The term referred to the practice of hiding a secret flask in the leg of one's boot. Before that, the bootleg had been used to hide knives and daggers. It was a handy receptacle for concealed carry. For John Kelly, though, the concealed receptacles would be his ice wagons. After talking to the bishop, John immediately set off to confer with his brother Ed.

In 1917, the Tennessee legislature did, indeed, enact the "bone-dry bill," and John Kelly did close his saloon. On April 6 of that year, just as he was laying the groundwork for his next move, the US entered the Great War in support of the Allies. Upward of nineteen thousand Tennesseans volunteered. All across the country, thousands of men went through basic training while thousands more worked on the logistics of moving tons of vehicles, munitions, food, and supplies across the ocean. To meet the demands of war, the US introduced rationing, with "meatless

Tuesdays" and "wheatless Wednesdays," as well as a wartime ban on alcohol production to save grain.

Seizing this opportunity, temperance advocates in Congress drew up the Eighteenth Amendment to ban all alcohol for a period of seven years. During the following eleven months, as the amendment was debated in forty-eight state legislatures, these same advocates managed to eliminate the seven-year time limit and replace it with a permanent ban.

Just as John had foreseen, Congress soon enacted the Selective Service Act and drafted nearly three million men into military service, including more than sixty thousand additional Tennesseans. Due to his status as a single parent, John received a deferment, so he set aside what funds he could to purchase Liberty Bonds in support of the troops. By this point, though, his savings were severely depleted. He was pinning all his hopes on his liquor trade.

His plan succeeded, for despite its horrors, the Great War brought rip-roaring prosperity to Tennessee. There was the new Alcoa aluminum plant in the east and the DuPont munitions factory near Nashville. Thousands of Tennesseans were finding work, and the money was flowing. People could afford to satisfy their taste for fine whiskey.

John and his brother Ed discussed the ice delivery idea at length, and they were both convinced it would work. John would continue selling the inventory stored in his attic. When that was gone, he would buy crates of legal liquor in Kentucky, storing them in the Kelly and Sons warehouse in Nashville, hidden among the blocks of ice. Each week, when they loaded their ice wagons to make deliveries, the liquor would be slipped in with the orders and passed discreetly to customers along the route. The ice bills at the first of each month would include the liquor cost, and no one would be the wiser. At least, that's what John hoped.

His first whiskey supplier was his friend Lem Motlow, who'd inherited the Jack Daniel's distillery from his uncle. Years earlier, Captain Jack had opened a large liquor warehouse in Hopkinsville, Kentucky, to compete with rival distillers in the Bluegrass region, and later he'd opened one in St. Louis as well. Now John was delighted to buy his friend's whiskey. Since Jack Daniel's death, John had been seeing a lot more of Motlow, and their friendship had deepened. Lem's Hopkinsville warehouse lay just seventy miles north of Nashville, so John made numerous trips to load up his Packard touring sedan with smooth, rich Old No. 7 whiskey. Then, early in May 1917, John traveled farther north toward Louisville in search of other types of liquor to fulfill his customers' requests.

Usually he took the train, but this time he drove, hoping to bring back a liquid cargo. He felt eager and optimistic as he followed the western route of the new Dixie Highway. The ambitious thoroughfare would eventually run from Chicago through Nashville all the way to Miami, and already the letters *DH* had been freshly painted in red and white on the roadside utility poles. At this early stage, however, the Dixie Highway was little more than a linkage of country roads—not all sections had even been paved—but John didn't need road signs to find his way to Louisville. He was headed for the Kentucky Derby.

John had been attending the Derby at Churchill Downs since he was old enough to ride the train. In the early twentieth century, horse racing was as popular as football is today, and the Kentucky Derby was its Super Bowl. Millionaires came from New York, Philadelphia, and Chicago to see their champion steeds compete. Some even built mansions in the area to be closer to the track.

John loved horse races. From early boyhood, he'd taken care of his father's ice wagon horses, feeding and grooming them, and cleaning their stalls. He and his father were both huge race fans. Maybe their passion for the sport was borne in their Irish genes. The songs and myths of Ireland were full of tales of heroic horses, and the Irish had been racing their steeds as early as the third century. The Irish were and still are a horse-loving people.

Of course, horse racing had always been a central occupation in Tennessee as well. Since 1807, when horse breeder John Harding established Belle Meade Plantation near Nashville, the state of Tennessee had led the nation in horse breeding and racing. Harding's son, William Giles Harding, built Belle Meade into a world-renowned Thoroughbred stud farm, and his stud Iroquois was the first American-bred horse to win the prestigious Epsom Derby in England. (Those in the know say almost every famous racehorse, including those that have won the Kentucky Derby such as Secretariat, since 1890 can be traced back to the Belle Meade stud farm.)[10]

John knew all the Nashville tracks, from the old Burns Island track flooded by the Cumberland River to the newer West Side Park track built on higher ground. By the early 1900s, a dozen tracks were operating in Tennessee, and he attended the races as often as work allowed. But in 1906, two years after he bought his saloon, the state legislature passed an anti-betting law that effectively ended horse racing in Tennessee. A short distance to the north, however, Kentucky welcomed the gambling dollars of the wealthy Eastern millionaires, and the center of horse racing migrated across the state border into Bluegrass country. When John needed a new supply of good liquor, naturally he combined his forays to Kentucky distilleries with visits to the racetracks.

As a resident of Tennessee, his mission to buy Kentucky whiskey was a delicate one. It might be tricky to strike deals that would pass legal muster, and with his money so tight, he had to negotiate the best possible terms.

When he visited Louisville bars and distilleries, John's tall, handsome appearance and lively sense of humor put people at ease, and he quickly made connections in the trade. Friends introduced him to George Garvin Brown, founder of Brown–Forman, the maker of Old Forester bourbon. Old Forester had been the first American whiskey sold in sealed glass bottles to ensure quality. Before that innovation, distilleries had commonly sold their spirits in barrels, to be bottled later—and sometimes diluted—by retail sellers. John felt comfortable buying Old Forester.

At the racetrack one day, John ran into an acquaintance from Ohio named Harry A. Brown. Harry worked in liquor distribution, and before the bone-dry law, John had often bought his wares. John liked Harry's straightforward manner, good business sense, and respect for excellent whiskey. The two men were close in age, and they got along well. Plus, Harry had contacts all over the Midwest. When John explained his ice delivery idea for selling liquor in Nashville, Harry got excited. As an Ohioan, he could serve as John's front man to make legal purchases. So they agreed to become partners. Harry would invest the money, and John would invest the sweat.

PART II

SMUGGLERS

Chapter 11

U-DRIVE-IT

When John's friends and former customers got word of the special ice deliveries, scores of them jumped at the chance to receive quality name brand liquor delivered regularly to their doors. Besides the obvious convenience, they found it far less risky than sneaking through back alleys to buy watered-down moonshine, especially with Mayor Gupton breathing down their necks. In short, John's home delivery of fine whiskey and ice was a formula for success.

By early 1918, he was making regular trips to Louisville to meet Harry Brown, and he soon saw that he would need more drivers to transport the liquor he was buying. But with the fiercely prohibitionist Mayor Gupton in charge of Nashville, the comings and goings of his drivers would need a good cover.

A couple of years earlier, John had read about a businessman named Joe Saunders in Omaha, Nebraska, who was renting Model Ts for ten cents a mile. Since few people could afford their own autos, Saunders was having success, and at the time, John had thought auto rental might be a great side business. Now he realized it would also be a great cover for his transport drivers. That spring he took out loans for four new Packards, and when the cars arrived in Nashville at the beginning of June, he put up a sign announcing the U-Drive-It Rental Car Company. The old horse stable had never seen such splendor.

To prove the legitimacy of his rental business, John ran ads in the local papers, and he gained a steady trickle of customers. His actual intent, of course, was to disguise the expansion of his liquor-running fleet. With that in mind, he hired four trustworthy new drivers and outfitted them with fine suits, hats, and ties. These drivers posed as rental customers so that, hopefully, their comings and goings would appear normal.

John had his men removed the Packards' back seats so they could stack up more liquor crates, which they concealed under car seat blankets. These heavy wool blankets were in common use, owing to the draftiness of early automobiles, so they would appear normal at a casual glance. Still, John instructed his drivers to take every precaution. They would drive at night, change their routes often, and follow the least-used lanes and wagon roads.

The most dangerous part would be driving into Nashville under the eyes of Mayor Gupton's police force. Thankfully, John had many customers on the police force, but he warned his drivers to stay alert. In the predawn hours, they would drive slowly through the farmlands north of Nashville, and then shut off their headlights to cross the Cumberland River on one of the city's two bridges. From there, the vehicles would roll down to the riverbank where Kelly and Sons kept their warehouse. John or Ed would open the doors to let them park inside, and amid the cold, gleaming blocks of ice, they would unload the goods.

It wasn't long before the U-Drive-It Rental Car Company was humming, and as long as liquor remained legal in Kentucky, John's trade did well, but the air was full of talk of the Eighteenth

Amendment and a coming nationwide ban. As a hedge against that day, distillers were ramping up production to new heights.

Like the distilleries, John and Harry were also planning ahead. Kelly and Sons rented extra warehouse space around Nashville and arranged for storage in other towns. In these secret caches, they stockpiled as much extra whiskey as they could afford. Unloading crates one day, John joked that the liquor trade was like the course of true love: it never did run smoothly.

And neither did the world's history in those momentous years of war. Historians estimate that fifty million people died of influenza between 1918–1919 during a global pandemic, spread in part by the movements of soldiers. And when the Great War finally shuddered to a halt on November 11, 1918, more than seventeen million people had died in battle, including thirty-four thousand Tennessee soldiers. Europe was left impoverished, its citizens demoralized, its borders redrawn, and the world was changed forever.

Early the following year, in 1919, Nebraska became the thirty-sixth state to ratify the Eighteenth Amendment, and on October 27, Congress passed the Volstead Act to put it into effect, making Prohibition the law of the land. As a result, John's sources of legal Kentucky whiskey dried up overnight.

Chapter 12

A WILD NEW DECADE DAWNS

As 1920 opened, serious tensions were straining the European peace. With the emergence of fascism and communism, all major powers were rearming with ever-more lethal weapons. Here at home, the war-driven economic boom had collapsed, leading to a postwar recession. John's morning newspapers were full of talk of strikes, riots, conspiracy theories, and a growing fear of "Reds."

In Nashville, Anne Dallas Dudley and her suffragettes finally convinced the state legislature to ratify the Nineteenth Amendment, and that August, Tennessee became the last state needed to give women the vote. But the recession and job loss were having a dreary effect on the city's life. Just when people needed a lift, all the Kentucky distilleries had shut down, and bonded whiskey grew so scarce and expensive that only the affluent could afford it.

Then in November, Warren G. Harding was elected US president on a campaign promise of a "return to normalcy." Right after he took office, his Republican Congress quickly slashed taxes, abolished wartime controls, restricted immigration, and set high tariffs to protect American industry. Though these policies would eventually lead to trade wars with Europe and an economic crash, they had the short-term effect of jump-starting a frenzied new prosperity.

In almost no time, demand for good liquor shot up as fast as the bubbly new economy, and Nashville's many new speakeasies were increasing their orders weekly. Kelly and Sons' home delivery service had become everyone's favorite supplier, and John felt gratified that he and Harry Brown had shown the foresight to stockpile a good supply. The ice wagons were still making normal deliveries, but the secret caches were dwindling fast. So John and Harry began an urgent search for new sources. While Harry worked his contacts in Kentucky, Illinois, Indiana, and Ohio, John scouted along the porous seacoast of the South.

In New Orleans, John learned of a thriving liquor trade in the Bahamas. To find the right supplier, he knew he'd have to visit the islands in person. In 1921, he caught a train to Miami, where he booked a flight to Nassau with the brand-new Aeromarine West Indies Airways, one of the earliest commercial airlines in the country.

As the plane rose above Florida's aquamarine waters, John gazed out the side window, buoyant and excited. He sensed he was on the verge of something big. In fact, the entire country was on the verge of what would come to be called the Roaring Twenties.

The decade of the 1920s marked a period of rampant affluence in the US—and rapid change. There were technological advances in virtually every field. New medical discoveries included insulin, penicillin, and the first antitoxin for tetanus. Rail lines expanded their routes, and sleek new ocean liners plied the seas. Before long, commercial airlines cropped up in every major city, and faster airplanes became available.

But more than anything else, travel by car changed the face of America. The US auto industry produced new and improved models every year through the 1920s. In every state, roads and bridges had to be redesigned to carry auto traffic. The first standardized road signs appeared, along with the first traffic lights and the first "Good Gulf Gasoline" service stations with electrically powered pumps.

As corporate profits rose, so did wages, and for the first time, retailers began to advertise installment plan buying. Suddenly, ordinary working people could buy cars, refrigerators, washing machines, vacuum cleaners, furniture, even life insurance—items that previously only the wealthy could afford. Now, just about anyone with a job could enjoy immediate gratification, and the easy credit sent America on a wild spending spree.

All this was good news for John's business, of course. Along with new radios, phonographs, and tickets to see Charlie Chaplin in the movies, people were going out more to restaurants and nightclubs, dancing to the new upbeat tempos of jazz and ragtime. Nashville speakeasies had never been so jubilant. If only John could meet the right dealer in Nassau, he felt sure that Kelly and Sons would prosper.

He wasn't yet worried about the mounting speculation in the stock market, which seemed to rise higher every day. People wanted to celebrate, and so did he. Just about everyone he knew thought Prohibition was a stupid mistake. No wonder it became the most widely flouted law in US history.

John had no way of foreseeing how the people's contempt for one law would lead to their general contempt for all laws. He couldn't guess how skyrocketing corporate profits would generate greed and white-collar corruption. Nor could he anticipate the

Harding administration's many scandals, involving some of the most flagrant cases of political bribery ever.[11]

Anything Goes was Cole Porter's musical portrayal of this period. Speakeasies operated openly. Jazz bands played to packed crowds every night, and the booze flowed like nectar. Retailers sold portable stills, and people made "bathtub gin" at home. Errol Flynn, a popular movie star, was reported to have made gin in the barbershop of his hotel, and even President Harding kept a personal liquor supply in the White House.

Over the course of the 1920s, the liquor trade would grow incredibly lucrative. With so much money in circulation, it was easy to understand why everyone felt optimistic.

Chapter 13

THE BAHAMA QUEEN

Warm, muggy breezes rattled the palm trees as John's plane touched down on a sandy grass strip near Nassau, The Bahamas. In 1921, The Bahamas was still under British rule, and Nassau had no official airport as yet. Though the landing was bumpy, John felt lighthearted. He was thirty-eight years old, and this was his first trip to a foreign country—the first of many to come.

He climbed out of the plane, stretched his long legs, and smiled. Impossibly blue waters lapped the white beach, and hummingbirds flitted around exotic pink and yellow blossoms.

Nassau was a small town with wide, sandy streets and mostly run-down single-story buildings. Nonetheless, it was teeming with visitors, and since Prohibition, many new hotels had sprung up. John's contacts in Miami had recommended the Colonial Hotel at the city's center, so he found his way there, checked in, and freshened up. After a few cocktails and casual conversation at the hotel bar, he was strolling along Bay Street in a light summer suit and bow tie, topped off with a smart straw boater. He had detailed instructions on how to purchase the whiskey that was needed to supply his thirsty customers back in Nashville.

Bay Street had been dubbed "Booze Avenue," and John could see why. It was lined with bars and liquor stores. More like shanties than saloons, these rickety, sun-bleached structures had never seen a lick of paint, yet some of them housed the agents of major distilleries and exporters, and their stockrooms held close to ten million dollars' worth of whiskey—all legal under British law.

When John reached Market Street, he turned south and looked for the office of Haig and McTavish, which the bartender at the Colonial had recommended. Their agent, Cleo Lythgoe, was the best in town, the bartender had assured him.

"Don't be put off that she's a woman," the barkeep had said. "Cleo's the queen of the Bahamas rumrunners."

The woman's real name was Gertrude. Although she was of English and Scottish descent, she'd picked up the nickname "Cleo" because she had the dark, exotic looks of Cleopatra. When strangers quizzed her about where she was from, she sometimes said Egypt, or India, or South America, because she liked to remain elusive. Tall and slender, in her early thirties, she had long, raven-black waves that shimmered in sunlight, and her enormous eyes smoldered. John soon discovered she had a keen business mind as well.

Like John, Cleo had lost her mother at a tender age, and she'd grown up working to earn her keep. Born in Ohio, she'd traveled widely and worked in California, New York, and London. When her British employer, Haig and McTavish, saw the opportunities opened up by the Volstead Act, they started exporting liquor through The Bahamas, and Cleo's business savvy earned her the assignment. She had set up shop on

Market Street, and from there, she oversaw the warehouses, made sales, and arranged for shipments.

Rough-and-tumble Nassau couldn't have been an easy place for a beautiful young woman to live alone, but Cleo possessed an iron will, and she could show spectacular fury when needed. A story was going around that when a certain gentleman insulted her liquor and her morals, she tracked him down at a barbershop and hauled him to her office with his face still lathered for a shave. There she warned him in blunt terms that she would put a bullet in his chest if he insulted her again.

Another time, she'd awakened in the night to find an intoxicated stranger sitting on the edge of her bed, reaching under the mosquito netting to fondle her. She sat up and thrust her hand under the pillow as if reaching for a hidden gun. In truth, she was unarmed and defenseless, but her fierce attitude and blistering words drove the man away.

John found her to be a formidable negotiator, but in the end, she sold him top-quality merchandise at a fair price. John also found her enchanting. Five years his junior, she was a cultivated woman who loved good books, good music, and the latest fashions. He'd heard that any man who made a pass at her was likely to find a pistol jammed in his ribs. She must have made an exception for the attractive, silver-haired John because when he invited her to dinner that night to celebrate their agreement, she accepted.

They met in the lavish dining room of the Colonial Hotel, and after John had ordered their dinner, they settled into easy conversation. First, Cleo regaled him with tales of her adventures in Hawaii, Paris, San Francisco, and New York. In turn, he told her about his children back in Nashville, his saloon and ice businesses, and his dreams. They both shared a taste for good food and

French wine, as well as a passion for horse racing. It was clear they enjoyed each other's company.

After a few drinks, she confided in him about the opposition she'd faced when she first arrived in Nassau. It seemed everyone viewed her as either a fly-by-night adventuress or an American spy. When she applied for her wholesale liquor license, the authorities informed her that no license had ever been granted to a female. But since there was no law against it, she persisted with her application. Just before the licensing board met, she spoke with the court clerk and found the Haig and McTavish license had been granted in the name of her drunken male associate. She rushed out and found him in a bar, waving the license and boasting that Cleo was only his typist. After she lambasted him with a few sharp words, he rose, shamefaced, and followed her back to the courthouse to correct the mistake.

She'd had just as much trouble finding buyers because, as a lady of taste, she did not like to fraternize in coarse company. Nor could she take potential clients to the lewd ceremonial sun dances on the beach, where young Bahamian women swayed almost naked around bonfires. She'd had even more trouble dealing with the cutthroat shippers who'd tried to take advantage of her supposed feminine gullibility.

Finally, after months of idling on her balcony, watching the boisterous drinking orgies at the Lucerne Hotel across the street, she'd made friends with the hotel owner, a woman everyone called "Mother." The Lucerne was dubbed "Bootleggers Headquarters" because of the salty mix of sea captains, middlemen, rogues, and opportunists who inhabited the place. The well-known Bronfman family of Canada had an agent there, as did many US bootleggers. Once Mother verified that the dark-haired American "gypsy" was not a spy, she began to help Cleo make contacts. In due course,

Cleo's expertise and honest hard work led to a large, well-satisfied clientele.

When John asked what life was like in Nassau, Cleo rolled her eyes. Keep a wary lookout, she cautioned. Nassau's denizens were as lawless and greedy as prospectors in the old Gold Rush. With all the booze sloshing around, men often reeled through the streets looking for a fight, and even though guns were supposedly illegal, shoot-outs were common, as were knife fights and theft.

Bootleggers dealt in cash, and thousand-dollar bills floated as freely in Nassau as fivers on the mainland. It's been said of that time that no matter how large the denomination, a Nassau bartender could always change it. Cleo pointed out the various millionaires in the dining room that evening and described how they'd earned their nefarious wealth. Then she gave John a dazzling smile and promised that, one day, she'd be pointing him out as a millionaire. John only shook his head and laughed.

Before they parted, she referred John to a shipper he could trust, a man who would see John's goods safely to the Florida coast. This shipper happened to be a dear friend of hers, the famous rumrunner Bill McCoy.

Chapter 14

THE REAL MCCOY

Although the phrase "the real McCoy," originated from "the real Mackay," an 1870 slogan used by G. Mackay & Co. Ltd., whisky distillers in Scotland, the moniker became the calling card of American's premier smuggler of fine quality whiskey, Bill McCoy. McCoy often referred to himself as "The Real McCoy"—because it was well-known that he never watered down the alcohol he sold.

Born in Syracuse, New York, in 1877, William Frederick "Bill" McCoy grew up sailing, and he loved boats of all kinds. He graduated first in his class from the Pennsylvania Nautical School, then served as mate and quartermaster on various commercial vessels. In 1898, he was serving on a steamer in Havana, Cuba, when the USS *Maine* exploded, launching the Spanish–American War.

Two years later, when Bill was twenty-three, his family moved to the small Florida town of Holly Hill, on the Halifax River just north of Daytona Beach. There, he and his brother, Ben, set up a boatyard with a motorboat excursion and freight service. In less than ten years, their reputation for excellence had grown to the point that they were building luxury yachts for Andrew Carnegie, the Vanderbilts, and other Eastern millionaires.

But like so many others, they fell on hard times in the recession following World War I, and when a smuggler offered Bill a hundred dollars to sail a cargo of liquor from Nassau to Georgia, Bill was tempted. Though he wasn't much of a drinker, he believed that Prohibition was an unfair intrusion on personal privacy.

Ultimately, he turned the offer down and decided to become a smuggler himself. Just months before John Kelly made his first trip to Nassau, Bill had scraped together the last of his savings to buy a ninety-foot schooner called the *Henry L. Marshall*. From Florida, he sailed into Nassau Harbor and bought fifteen hundred cases of fine imported whiskey from Cleo Lythgoe. Three days later, he unloaded his cargo on the Georgia coast for a huge profit.

After that trip, Bill McCoy was hooked. He hired a skipper for the *Marshall* and purchased a swift, 130-foot twin-masted schooner for himself called the *Arethusa*. To carry the largest possible load, he retrofitted her cargo hold, and he also installed a larger auxiliary motor. Always a clever and prudent man, he mounted a swivel machine gun on her prow, concealed under a hood, and he armed his crew and himself with smaller weapons. Once at sea, he kept a sharp watch for the authorities—and for pirates.

In the weeks that followed, he returned regularly to Nassau, picked up more cargo from Cleo's warehouse, and then sailed up the "Great Whiskey Way" as far north as Nantucket Island. Cleo must have liked his tanned, chiseled features, or perhaps it was his clever mind. He was forty-four, six-foot-two, with broad shoulders, steady eyes, and a voice like a foghorn. Cleo's magnetic qualities drew him as well, and the two of them became fast friends.

Bill pioneered the use of what he called "hams," triangular burlap sacks filled with a pyramid of six liquor bottles encased in salt. They were much easier to stack compactly below the ship's deck and easier to handle than traditional wooden liquor cases during a bumpy nighttime transfer at sea. If trouble arose approaching the shore, they would toss the hams overboard, where they would quickly sink out of sight, and days later, when the salt dissolved, they would float back to the surface and be successfully retrieved undamaged.

From experience, he knew that maritime law set the boundary for national waters at three miles off the coast so he anchored his ships just beyond that boundary where the Coast Guard had no jurisdiction. Then he sent prearranged signals to his customers on shore, and they motored out to pick up their orders.

"Come out anytime you want to," Bill told the public. "The law can't touch us here, and we'll be very glad to see you."

In no time, his ship became a virtual floating liquor store, and he welcomed reputable-looking buyers, though his armed crew kept up a careful guard. He displayed samples and encouraged tastings to prove that the liquor he sold was the good stuff, "the real McCoy."

In a few months, so many other smugglers were following his lead that the three-mile line became known as Rum Row. Some ships even hung poster-sized price lists over their gunwales to advertise their wares, and a strange new waterborne shopping took form. That year alone, Bill moved close to 175,000 cases of whiskey out of Nassau Harbor, and for every trip up the coast, he earned an estimated $300,000.

In the stories I heard growing up, John Kelly first met Bill McCoy in the lobby of the Colonial Hotel. Cleo introduced them, then ushered them to the table she'd reserved in the hotel dining room. Over a dinner of lobster and prawns, John explained the purchase he'd just made from Cleo, and Bill outlined his fee and his process. For the first shipment, he would anchor off the Florida coast near Daytona Beach, and John could motor out from the McCoys' Halifax River boatyard to pick up his goods. Bill even offered John the loan of a motorboat for his first run.

John liked Bill's frankness and generosity. They were only a few years apart in age, and they both came from immigrant Irish families. Bill's father had been a bricklayer, a workingman like James Kelly. Bill and John had both grown up developing strong work ethics. As they continued talking, John learned that Bill had never paid a bribe to anyone and that all the liquor he carried was unadulterated and safe. Both John and Bill considered themselves "honest lawbreakers." And like many men in Nassau, they both had a secret crush on the dark-eyed Cleo. That night at the Colonial Hotel, they settled their arrangements with a champagne toast, under the approving smile of their lovely hostess.

Back in Florida, John met Bill's brother, Ben McCoy, at the Halifax River boatyard. His loaner boat was a small runabout with gleaming varnished wood and a powerful new Evinrude outboard motor. For an hour or so, he practiced steering the boat up and down the river. Then at nightfall, he motored quietly out to the shore and waited. They'd already arranged the searchlight signal, three long flashes followed by a pause, then a long flash, a short flash, and a long flash. Bill told him this was Morse code for "OK."

The night was clear and starry, and a brisk wind was blowing up white caps in the choppy waves. John had never piloted a boat in the ocean, especially not a smuggler's boat, and he felt as jumpy as a cricket. When the signal came sometime after midnight, he jerked to attention, revved up his motor, and darted out through the surf. For a novice pilot in a small craft, three miles of rough ocean waves at night were quite a distance, and the *Arethusa* was running dark, so John had to use his own searchlight to find her.

Bill's crew had already lowered its fenders, so John eased his boat in and bumped against them. He tossed his bow and stern lines to the waiting deckhands, and when the runabout was made fast, he climbed aboard the yacht, where a laughing Bill McCoy was waiting to clap him on the back.

Together, they loaded John's cargo into the runabout, taking care to balance the load. Then Bill invited him to share a cocktail on deck. Under the brilliant canopy of stars, they toasted to each other's success, and as they sipped their mild gin rickeys, Bill waxed poetic about the smuggling life: "There was all the kick of gambling and the thrill of sport, and, besides these, there were the open sea and the boom of the wind against full sails, dawn coming out of the ocean, and nights under the rocking stars. These caught and held me most of all."[12]

John listened quietly, gazing into the night. The romance of the sea had caught his imagination too.

Chapter 15

MOTORBOATS AND MOTORCARS

After the exchange, John had his "rental" drivers take the Florida load back to Nashville while he went ahead on the train. During the long train ride home, he kept reliving the thrills of his midnight roller-coaster ride on the ocean. As soon as he reached his office, he told his brother Ed, "We need a boat."

By this time, Kelly and Sons' liquor sales were steadily rising, and Cleo had assured John she could deliver as much liquor as he wanted. The Nassau connection was solid gold. But he couldn't keep borrowing Bill McCoy's runabout.

Just before leaving Florida, John had looked at a boat Bill's brother, Ben, had for sale, a nice, new twenty-six-foot mahogany model. It was a thing of beauty, and John was captivated. After looking the boat over, he'd gone straight to the Halifax Marina to check on a slip. Altogether, the cost of the boat plus slip fees would be pretty steep, but John felt Kelly and Sons could afford it. Back in Nashville, he would start setting aside part of his liquor profits to buy the boat.

At home, John's sons and little daughter were growing fast, and he was able to place them all in good schools. He also hired a cook to help the household maid who'd been with him all these years. The Kellys almost always spent Sundays together. Early service at the cathedral was followed by a big family lunch with John's brothers and sisters and their families. Mary and Nellie Clare would take turns cooking. John, Ed, and Will would talk politics, and the kids would play football in the yard. At home later that night, John and his children would gather around the radio to listen to favorite shows. That winter they particularly enjoyed the comic songs on the popular radio program *The Happiness Boys*. Yes, Sundays were grand.

The rest of the week, John was meeting customers, making new contacts, and negotiating deals, while brother Ed ran the day-to-day operations. John was still meeting friends at the horse races in Louisville, and when possible, he bought inventory from his former Kentucky suppliers. His fleet of rental Packards went through tires and parts so fast that he and Ed set up their own auto repair shop in the horse stable.

Around this time, John bought his first ice delivery truck, a 1922 Mack with the revolutionary drive-shaft technology instead of the usual chain drive. The Mack was faster and more powerful than the Ford models of that year, and John viewed it as a good investment. Already, he could envision a day when Kelly and Sons would no longer use horse-drawn wagons at all.

He hired skilled mechanics to maintain the new truck and to modify his rental fleet for transport duty. Of course, his drivers had to be mechanics too. The autos of those years suffered numerous breakdowns, and John's drivers had to be able to change a tire in under five minutes, replace a fan belt, patch a leaky radiator, and diagnose a valve problem by its sound.

A liquor runner's vehicle had to be extremely specialized. It needed a powerful engine, extra-strong suspension, large fuel tanks, and plenty of well-concealed cargo space. It had to be durable, solidly built, and, most important, it had to be fast. Everywhere John's drivers traveled now, they encountered police patrols, and the police had fast cars too. Another liquor runner John knew had nearly died in a crash after being chased for miles by the police.

John's strategy was to dress his drivers well, drive at moderate speeds, and stay on the main roads along with other normal traffic. They no longer used the back roads, which were often watched now by police and hijackers alike. John's mechanics customized his rental fleet to keep the goods well hidden, and they regularly polished the cars to a high gloss. At roadblocks, John told his drivers to remain calm and courteous, always with a ready explanation for their trips. So far, the U-Drive-It auto rental cover had kept his men safe.

It wasn't long before John returned to Florida to buy his exquisite mahogany motorboat. Each time he motored out of the Halifax Marina, he felt like a character in Rudyard Kipling's novel *Captains Courageous*. On nights when he rendezvoused with Bill McCoy, they always shared a light cocktail on deck and a genial talk. Once Bill brought Cleo along, and the three of them had a fine reunion. Cleo brought the news from Nassau, which was growing busier and more unruly by the day. She invited John to come see her new warehouse, and he promised that he would.

After a few weeks, John felt like an old hand at the tiller of his boat. He learned to reverse, maneuver in close quarters, turn on a dime, and dock with ease. He felt ready for most any situation—until the night the tropical storm hit. He'd already picked up his load and was heading back, riding low in the water due to the weight, when the first winds struck. He was two miles out from shore, and this was no ordinary summer squall but a real gale-force tempest. The waves rose quickly. From where John sat, they looked like mountains. Soon he was spinning sideways and pitching off course. In a matter of minutes, his cockpit was swamped, and loose "hams" of whiskey were sloshing against his legs. The tiller felt like a wild creature in his hands, and it was all he could do to hold on.

Rain blew in his face, obscuring the lights on shore. He hunkered over his compass and wrestled the tiller, trying to steer west, not knowing from one minute to the next whether his boat might capsize. If he fell into these raging waves, he would surely drown. He prayed aloud for deliverance.

When he finally managed to reach the marina, he crossed himself and said a prayer of gratitude. Then he decided on the spot to sell the "damned boat" and hire someone else to pick up his cargo at sea.

Chapter 16

MCCOY LEAVES THE TRADE

Not long after John's ill-fated boat trip, Bill McCoy also ran into a patch of trouble. His hired skipper was sailing the *Marshall* off the New Jersey coast when she drifted inside the three-mile line and was seized by the Coast Guard, along with fourteen hundred cases of whiskey. This was a costly mistake, and when Bill was identified as the owner, he became a wanted man.

Within days, he closed down his Florida boatyard and moved lock, stock, and barrel. Always a step ahead of other liquor runners, Bill chose a quiet fishing village in the French colony of St. Pierre Island, off the eastern coast of Canada. This put him closer to the north end of Rum Row and the red-hot market of New York City. St. Pierre was a French territory, beyond US jurisdiction, and export taxes were considerably lower than in The Bahamas. To prevent any more surprises, Bill registered the *Arethusa* under French sovereignty and renamed her the *Marie Celeste* so the US Coast Guard couldn't board her at sea. He had always been a leader in the bootlegging trade, and others soon followed his move. St. Pierre grew into one of the most successful smuggling ports of the era.

By that autumn, Rum Row had become so crowded with competitors that, at night, their flotilla looked like a waterborne city. Some ships flew banners inviting customers to wild parties with prostitutes, and every crew traveled heavily armed to ward off hijackers.

Still trying to evade the law, Bill moved his headquarters a second time that year, back to Nassau, and he renamed his ship the *Tomoka*. Cleo helped him arrange for a Nassau broker to temporarily buy the schooner, register her as a British vessel, and then sell her back to Bill for the same price, minus an ample commission. For a while, Bill McCoy, the so-called King of Rum Row, no longer anchored his ship in the Row at all. Instead, he delivered cargo to other anchored vessels, then cruised straight back to the safety of Nassau Harbor.

To maintain his profits, he bought two more ships and then hired skippers to sail them. Regrettably, the new men lacked Bill's seagoing know-how. One ship was seized by the Coast Guard, and the other was wrecked in a storm. Both were carrying valuable cargoes, and by year's end, those losses pushed Bill to the edge of bankruptcy.

Rum Row's enormous fleet now stretched in a dense, ever-present line from the tip of Florida to the Gulf of Maine, and coastal fishermen earned far more from shuttling liquor to shore than from catching fish. Competition was fierce and not always honorable. Every kind of craft would zoom out under the cover of night to pick up illicit orders.

Yet Bill McCoy, the man who'd invented Rum Row, was on the verge of ruin. Desperate for cash, he sailed the *Tomoka* himself in 1923 and anchored off the coast of New Jersey, a risk he'd vowed never to take again. Luckily, his cargo sold out in two days, and since he encountered no difficulty, he repeated the trip several more times. His daring paid off. Soon flush with cash, his reputation as King of the Row was restored—until one peaceful night in November.

Bill had anchored the *Tomoka* six and a half miles off the coast of Sea Bright, New Jersey, well outside the three-mile limit. In placid seas just before daybreak, he and his crew were unloading their last two hundred cases when a Coast Guard cutter hailed them and approached to board. Bill shouted angry protests. The *Tomoka* was flying a British flag in international waters, and this was a clear violation of maritime law. But his arguments made no difference. The Coast Guard captain seemed determined to arrest the famous Bill McCoy.

When the agents climbed on deck and tried to seize Bill's goods, a fistfight broke out. Impulsively, Bill hoisted his sails and got underway with the agents still aboard. The cutter pursued him, firing two six-pounder shots over his bow, and Bill realized he couldn't outrun their steam-powered engines. Biting back his fury, he dropped his sails and surrendered. He was arrested on the spot, and his ship was seized. Later, when the British protested, the US authorities justified their action on a technicality in a maritime act dating from 1790. Bill never saw the *Tomoka* again.

For the next two years, he remained free on bail fighting his case. In the end, he served nine months in a low-security hotel. When he saw how many rival groups were taking over the liquor trade, he moved back to Florida to build boats again with his brother. John Kelly would never find such an "honest lawbreaker" again.

Chapter 17

A PRIVATE LUMBER TRAIN

Bill McCoy's exit from the trade meant that John had to find a new skipper to transport his goods from Cleo's Nassau warehouse. He ventured to Florida's western coast, to a town just north of Tampa with a reputation for easy access to liquor. The place was Ybor City, the "cigar-rolling capital of the world." This village of blossoming vines, charming brick buildings, and wrought-iron balconies was a Mafia hotbed. While thousands of skilled artisans were hand-rolling a million fine cigars each year, the speakeasies along Seventh Avenue overflowed with liquor, gambling, and cash. John talked to a few bartenders and bought a few boxes of cigars, but Ybor City's pervasive graft disturbed him.

Later that summer, Cleo arranged for him to meet a new Bahamian shipper at a rendezvous site off the coast of South Carolina. The Lowcountry shoreline was a ragged maze of marshes, estuaries, and small islands, impossible to patrol and ideal for clandestine meetings. Liquor flowed through that shoreline as freely as the tides. Cleo said the Bahamians would pose as fishermen motoring their small craft up the mouth of the Cooper River, south of Charleston Harbor.

For this trip, John organized a new means of land transport. He bought a load of lumber in Charleston, then chartered a private freight train to carry it to Nashville via the Southern Railway. He sent trusted employees to travel with the lumber. At a certain point, his crew chief paid the train engineer to leave the main line and pull onto a remote siding parallel to the Cooper River. Of course the engineer knew what was happening, but he was paid well for his silence. In the 1920s, thousands of people along the coast earned cash from the liquor trade.

At the appointed hour, the fishing skiff glided upriver and nosed into the bank near the waiting train. John's crew chief hopped on deck, opened one of the crates, and tasted a bottle at random to make sure it was the genuine article. Then the crew helped the Bahamians offload the cargo and conceal it among the stacks of lumber in the freight cars. Money changed hands, then everyone tipped their hats and quietly parted company.

When the train approached Nashville, the crew chief directed the engineer to stop once again on an out-of-the-way siding, where Ed was waiting with the new Mack truck. The crew transferred the liquor crates, and Ed drove them quietly into Nashville, while the crew chief continued on the train to Union Station to have John's lumber unloaded under the eye of the customs inspector. Since Nashville's construction boom was in full swing, John had little trouble selling his lumber, adding a nice bonus to his profit.

This system worked so well that he sent his crew back several more times, though he couldn't always depend on the same shippers. The Coast Guard launched a major crackdown in 1924, deploying extra cutters to cruise the coast and arrest anyone found carrying liquor inside the maritime limit. John lost more than one supplier that way.

But Rum Row responded with heightened vigilance. The enterprising Bronfman family of Canada owned many ships in the Row, and their patriarch, Samuel Bronfman, bought private radio stations to keep in touch with his skippers about Coast Guard movements.[13] Whenever a Coast Guard cutter appeared, some designated captain would run out to sea and send a distress call, and the Coast Guard was obligated to respond. All the while, Rum Row kept expanding.

Chapter 18

HARRY BROWN AND GEORGE REMUS

During the time John had been venturing south to The Bahamas, his partner Harry Brown had been talking to his contacts in the central states of Kentucky, Illinois, Indiana, and Ohio. In a curious twist, Harry's brother-in-law, George Remus, was on his way to becoming one of the nation's premier suppliers of fine bonded whiskey.

How Remus earned the title "King of the Bootleggers" is a peculiar tale. He was a son of poor immigrants like John Kelly, and by sheer dint of effort and ambition, he became a licensed pharmacist, then an attorney. Those two professions put him in the ideal spot to take advantage of a loophole in the Volstead Act.

While living in Chicago, he'd enjoyed a lucrative criminal law practice defending bootleggers, and he was amazed by the large sums of cash they carried. But George Remus was a careful man. His first step was to study the language of the law. The Volstead Act stated that inventories of liquor purchased or distilled before Prohibition were private property. They could neither be confiscated nor destroyed, merely impounded. Further, the inventory owners could legally sell "warehouse receipts" for their stock. In other words, though they couldn't transport the booze, on paper they could sell it.

Remus knew the warehoused inventories in the Midwest amounted to hundreds of millions of gallons of aged and bonded liquor, but how could he get the booze out of impoundment without risk? He continued scouring the law. That's when he discovered the loophole for "medicinal purposes." The law permitted physicians to prescribe liquor to treat illness, and distilleries could continue to manufacture it for that purpose. The so-called medicinal liquor could be withdrawn from an impounded warehouse by obtaining a government permit.

Now Remus had his plan! As a licensed pharmacist, he would obtain withdrawal permits for medicinal liquor, then sell it under the table. The plan sounded good in theory, but Remus had no experience in crime, and he soon ran afoul both of the Chicago bosses and the law. He was a fast learner, though, and he still believed his plan would work. So he dissolved his legal practice and moved to Cincinnati, Ohio, a major distilling center before Prohibition.

At this stage, Remus began to think big. No longer would he simply play the pharmacist and withdraw other people's inventory. With the wealth he'd earned as a lawyer, he set about buying as many Cincinnati distilleries as possible. He also hired their master distillers to continue making fine whiskey under the cover of the medicinal loophole. In addition, he bought several wholesale drug companies. From now on, he would take full control of manufacture and distribution of medicinal liquor to the masses. All he needed was an endless supply of government withdrawal permits.

Remus was lucky in his timing. The US government had never been more corrupt. Just as officials were dedicating the new Lincoln Memorial in 1922, newspaper headlines exposed the Teapot Dome Scandal, widely regarded as the most sensational scandal in US politics before Watergate. Although Wall Street had praised President Harding's 1920 campaign promise of "less government in business and more business in government," members of his administration were enriching themselves with graft.

It appeared that Harding's secretary of the interior, Albert Bacon Fall, had secretly granted exclusive leases of Wyoming's vital Teapot Dome petroleum reserves to Harry Sinclair of Mammoth Oil Company at below-market rates with no competitive bidding. When the Senate discovered proof that Secretary Fall had taken bribes, he became the first member of a US cabinet to go to prison. Oddly, though, no Mammoth executive was ever charged, and Harry Sinclair went on to found Sinclair Oil Company.

Along with the Teapot Dome Scandal, Harding's lax oversight spawned corruption in many other areas, including the Justice Department, which handled the issuance of liquor withdrawal permits.

Remus's lawyer arranged for Remus to meet a DOJ representative named Jesse Smith, a close friend and constant companion of the US attorney general. At the Commodore Hotel in New York, Smith promised not only to deliver as many authentic withdrawal permits as Remus wanted, complete with genuine signatures, he would also protect Remus from prosecution.

"If you're arrested, you'll never be indicted," Smith said. "No one will serve time in the penitentiary."

Smith's fee would be $50,000 for protection, plus a sliding scale of $1.50 to $2.50 per case for each liquor withdrawal permit, depending on shipment size. Remus didn't need to calculate.

Compared to the profits he stood to make, this bribe was well within bounds. He paid Smith's fee, and they smoked cigars to celebrate.

Remus quickly began withdrawing his liquor and transporting it to his drug wholesale companies. Then he hired stickup men to hijack his own trucks so he could sell his fine bonded whiskey to bootleggers—at premium prices. Before long, he was rolling in cash. With his pretty wife, Imogene, he settled into a grandiose Price Hill mansion in Cincinnati, where he filled the library with rare books and built an indoor Grecian swimming pool because Imogene liked to swim. He also bought an office building in downtown Cincinnati, which he rechristened the Remus Building. This was where Harry Brown brought John Kelly for a meeting.

Remus was a short, balding man, friendly and somewhat pompous, though a bit too plump to look well in his handsome suit. As he showed off the artwork in his expensively furnished conference room, John caught the trace of a German accent. Remus set out a few bottles of liquor and poured two glasses for Harry and John. "Please, be my guest."

When John lifted the glass to his lips, Harry Brown stood by, smiling. Harry had already sampled the wares, and he knew John would be pleased. Indeed, this was smooth, well-aged whiskey made by master distillers before Prohibition. John savored its oaky taste. The three men negotiated terms and made a deal. John's drivers would make their pickups at Remus's central warehouse, located on a fifty-acre spread west of Cincinnati called Death Valley Farm.

From then on, John's fleet of modified Packards made regular trips to Cincinnati, and so did liquor dealers from all over the eastern United States. Lines of vehicles were seen coming and going at Death Valley Farm at all hours, and to keep pace with demand,

Remus bought many more distilleries. When cash-strapped Lem Motlow was forced to sell the huge St. Louis warehouse that his uncle had opened earlier, Remus bought part interest in it, along with five other investors.

Remus also bought distilleries in Kentucky and around Lawrenceburg, Indiana, though he missed Lawrenceburg's famous Rossville Union Distillery, maker of a rich bourbon-style whiskey. Rossville Union was snapped up by the Bronfmans of Canada, and Sam Bronfman eventually consolidated several area distilleries under the name L.D.I., Lawrenceburg Distillers Indiana. The Bronfmans were extending their influence to all corners of the liquor trade, and John felt sure that one day he would meet them.

Shortly after Remus had purchased the Squibb Distillery in Lawrenceburg, Harry Brown came to John with good news and bad. The good news was, Remus had just made Harry president of the Squibb Distillery, which would ensure John all the bonded whiskey he needed for his supply chain in Nashville. Naturally, Harry couldn't pass up such a career opportunity. The bad news was, he would no longer have time to carry on his partnership with John. John wished him well, and they remained friends, but that left John alone to manage his supply chain.

Meanwhile, George Remus was living the high life. He and Imogene hosted an elaborate New Year's Eve party that year at what they were now calling their Marble Palace mansion. They invited one hundred of the area's most elite couples, and in a showy display of wealth, Remus gave each male guest a diamond stickpin and each of their wives a brand-new car. The liquor trade was roaring hotter than ever, and the stock market was still rising.

Then Remus took a tumble. His downfall began with a routine traffic stop of a man who was carrying a case of whiskey in his car. To avoid jail, the man told the police where he'd bought the whiskey and even drew a map to George Remus's Death Valley Farm. Federal agents raided the place, and George Remus was indicted on violations of the Volstead Act, along with several codefendants, including Harry Brown.

John Kelly was alarmed when he heard the news, but Harry told him not to worry because George had put the fix in. No doubt, he was referring to the protection money Remus had paid to Jesse Smith. Remus's lawyers soon got everyone released on bail. Even after they were convicted and sentenced to the federal penitentiary, Remus assured that they would get out on appeal. By then, he'd accumulated an estimated $40 million in liquor profits, and that year, he may have paid as much as a million in bribes. He paid Jesse Smith alone $50,000 more, then another $30,000.

But Remus may not have noticed how quickly Jesse Smith's health was failing or how despondent the man had grown in those last few months. While the case was still on appeal, Smith committed suicide. Despite Remus's battalion of expensive lawyers, all his legal stratagems eventually failed: Harry Brown and George Remus joined the other codefendants on a train bound for the federal penitentiary in Atlanta.[14]

Chapter 19

A TOUCH OF ROMANCE

By 1923, the Kelly family business was going exceptionally well. Few others in Nashville could match the quality of John's merchandise, or the discretion of his home delivery. His liquor sales were so profitable that he was able to buy more ice delivery trucks and retire all of his horse-drawn wagons. When he traveled on business, he wore tailored suits and carried a gold pocket watch, and he entertained associates in private clubs, treating them to thick Angus steaks and fine wines smuggled from France.

As the year drew to a close, John's life took a sudden surprising turn. He was attending a party with friends in Louisville when he caught sight of a young lady who was so luminous that he instantly asked the hostess to introduce him. The vivacious blue-eyed beauty was Ethel Bickham.

Petite and perky, only five-foot-two, Ethel was considered one of the prettiest young women in Louisville society. She had an infectious laugh and a witty sense of humor, and she was dressed in the newest "flapper" fashion, though she still wore her black hair long and full. Everyone found her adorable. And John was smitten.

On the surface, John and Ethel seemed an unlikely match. He was forty, and she was in her early twenties. His reputation in the liquor trade was well-known, while she was the respectable daughter of a prominent family. He viewed her as nothing less than a goddess, while she viewed him as an outlaw.

Nonetheless, John was determined to have her for his wife, and he set about wooing her with all the ingenuity he possessed. He sent her flowers and small gifts. He invited her to dine with him at the brand-new, sixteen-story Brown Hotel, just opened in Louisville at the staggering cost of four million dollars. The Brown's numerous restaurants were the latest rage, but Ethel Bickham said *no*.

John's friends couldn't believe such a streetwise man of the world could fall for a social debutante, and they found his courtship amusing. After all, he'd been enjoying his single life for many years. What would he even talk about with a girl nearly half his age? There was too much against the match, and many said it would never happen. But if they believed that, they didn't know John Kelly.

He continued to see Ethel socially, but she didn't change her mind about him, though from the glimmer in her eyes, John sometimes caught hints that she was softening. She refused his invitations to drive through the countryside or to stroll through Fountain Court, and though he met her often at parties, she refused all his many invitations until finally he hit upon an idea.

At great expense, he reserved box seats overlooking the finish line of the Kentucky Derby, a premium spot. The year 1924 marked the Derby's fiftieth running, and when he invited Ethel to join him in his box, she answered, "No Louisville girl would say no to that invitation."

(That ploy is still used today in Louisville, and it still works.)

John won twice that day at the races. He bet on Black Gold, the Derby winner. And his Irish charm finally won Ethel Bickham's heart.

As soon as she accepted his proposal of marriage, he commissioned builders to erect a fine new house in the green wooded hills just outside Nashville. It was the first house on what was then called the "concrete road," the first such road in Davidson County. The road's actual name was Woodmont Boulevard.

That summer, 1924, Ethel came to Nashville with her aunt to meet John's family. At first, William, Ed, Mary, and Nellie Clare raised their eyebrows at their brother's choice. A society girl barely out of finishing school, who couldn't even sew or boil an egg? They hardly knew how to speak to her. However, Ethel's warm wit and open nature soon made them see why John had fallen in love.

John's boys found her splendid, and as for Margaret, just turned thirteen, Ethel became the mother she'd never known. Before the end of the visit, Ethel asked Margaret to be her bridesmaid.

John's oldest son, Johnny, had just graduated from prep school at Montgomery Bell Academy, where he'd been a football star and set a school record for yardage. In the autumn, he would enter Millington College near Memphis. Jimmy, the younger boy, was the family daredevil, and he loved racing John's old Packard through the country lanes. During the summer break, John hired both boys to run errands for Kelly and Sons.

There was much to celebrate that year. Not only had John won Ethel's hand, but also Hilary Howse was reelected mayor. For John, that meant the speakeasies would be able to operate openly again. Printer's Alley was already rising like a phoenix from the ashes, and John bought more liquor to supply the swelling demand. As his marriage approached, his fortunes had never been brighter.

The wedding took place in Louisville at the Bickham's stately home. Their announcement ran in the society pages, and just about all of Louisville's elite were in attendance. During their honeymoon that autumn, John and Ethel traveled by private Pullman train compartments to cities all over the eastern US, and with his pretty new bride on his arm, John felt as happy as he had been in a long time.

Chapter 20

THE ST. LOUIS MILKING SCHEME

While George Remus was in prison, thirty-five people were charged with illegally withdrawing nearly nine hundred barrels of whiskey from the Jack Daniel's warehouse Remus and his partners owned in St. Louis. Since John's friend Lem Motlow had sold Remus the warehouse, Lem was called to St. Louis to give testimony. Then Lem ran into trouble.

The defendants were accused of using a process widely known as "milking." In this scheme, they allegedly gained access to Remus's impounded warehouse by getting one of their own men assigned as the guard. Once inside, they'd siphoned whiskey from the barrels through a long hose that ran outside to their trucks. They replaced the stolen whiskey with vinegar and water, leaving one barrel full of genuine Jack Daniel's for the inspection agent.

After Lem gave his testimony, he boarded the Louisville & Nashville night train to return home on St. Patrick's Day 1924. In the L&N club car, he joined some friends for drinks and a game of poker. The train seemed to take forever to leave Union Station in St. Louis. As time passed, Lem began to lose serious money at cards. To leave the table with grace, he claimed fatigue and ordered a porter to make up his bed. But Ed Wallis, the porter, said he couldn't make the bed until the train had left the station, due to local ordinances against trains competing with hotels.

As Lem's losses mounted, he asked for his bed again. But the train still hadn't moved, and the porter gave the same answer. The third time he asked, a heated argument broke out and now, totally frustrated, Lem drew his pistol. The conductor, Clarence Pullis, approached the men to intervene. But just at that moment, the train lurched out of the station and Lem's pistol accidentally went off, striking Pullis in the stomach. Pullis was rushed to a hospital in East St. Louis, where he died. Lem Motlow was charged with murder.

Family legend has it that one of Lem's first panicked calls was to John Kelly, asking for help. Lem needed a good lawyer in a hurry, and John assured him things would work out.

"Stay calm," John said. "You'll have the best lawyer I can find."

Immediately, John called a family friend, John Hooker Sr., and persuaded him to take the case.[15] Hooker was a partner in Nashville's preeminent law firm, which boasted some of the best legal minds in the South. This is how Seth Walker, an attorney for the L&N Railroad and former Speaker of the House in Tennessee, became affiliated with the case.

By year's end, Lem's first trial had ended in a hung jury. The second trial opened on December 4, 1924, before Circuit Court judge Henry Hamilton. The case had grown so complex that six additional lawyers had been called to assist Seth Walker. Among Lem's character witnesses was the sitting Tennessee governor, Austin Peay.

Attorney Seth Walker, a true legal mastermind, questioned the porter and key witness, Ed Wallis, about the L&N train pass he used to visit his girlfriend. The porter admitted the pass belonged to an acquaintance, and that he had "borrowed" it. Walker then asked the porter to read the words on the pass aloud. "Not transferrable," he read out.

At that, Walker turned to the jury and smiled. The porter had just admitted he'd stolen from his employer, the L&N Railroad, and Walker accused him of being a "fifty-cent crook." This strategy discredited Wallis's testimony, and when combined with the many witnesses attesting to Lem's good character, that won the day. The jury quickly voted to acquit him on December 10.

John treated Lem to dinner and hearty congratulations, but Lem was still so shaken he barely touched his food. He confided that, with two trials and seven lawyers, his legal fees had mounted to staggering heights. And now with his distillery shut down, he didn't have enough money to pay. "John, what should I do?" he asked.

John thought the problem over. "You've still got good whiskey in Lynchburg?"

"Sure," Lem said, "but it's impounded."

John nodded sagely. He then advised Lem to offer Mr. Hooker a share of the Lynchburg distillery as payment for the legal fees. "I'll talk to him," John said. "I believe he'll say yes, because one day Jack Daniel's will be a real jackpot."

The Jack Daniel's milking case was still going on in St. Louis when, at last, John Kelly's former partner, Harry Brown, finished his sentence and left the Atlanta penitentiary. He and John met for dinner and talked over the woes of George Remus, who was serving a longer sentence in the Cincinnati case on top of being embroiled now in the St. Louis milking case.

Before entering the Atlanta prison, Remus had taken the wise precaution of putting his vast wealth in the name of his wife, Imogene, so she could keep the operation running. But divulging this secret to a chummy fellow inmate was not so wise. The darkly handsome man, Franklin Dodge, was actually an undercover agent who'd grown greedy and corrupt. After hearing George's words, Dodge quickly resigned his post, left the prison, and started an affair with Imogene in order to get his hands on Remus's millions. Dodge and Imogene sold off many of Remus's holdings. When the imprisoned man found out, guards reported he cried like a child for hours.

Due to excessive newspaper coverage in St. Louis, the trial was moved to Indianapolis. When Remus took the stand, he glared at his wife, certain he was about to get justice. But justice proved elusive. Imogene's attorney pointed out that, since the two were still legally married, Remus could not testify against her. He shot to his feet, cursing. Before his disbelieving eyes, Imogene got off scot-free.

Remus made a deal for immunity in exchange for testifying against the thieves before the second grand jury. One of his St. Louis partners heard about the deal and offered Remus a share in a dog track as a bribe not to testify before the grand jury. He said the other dog track owner was a friend from Chicago, Al Capone. Remus eagerly accepted the bribe because he had no grudge against anyone but his wife, and he also needed the income. His sole purpose in testifying was to indict the faithless Imogene, but because she never signed the divorce papers, he couldn't testify against his wife.

After he appeared before the grand jury, Imogene was so furious at being indicated that she and Frank Dodge paid a gunman $15,000 to kill Remus. As luck would have it, the hit man was also a swindler, and he absconded with the money. More enraged than ever, Imogene tried to have Remus deported.

Her freedom didn't last, though. A few years later, Remus shot her dead in front of a crowd of horrified onlookers. Though he was acquitted on a plea of temporary insanity, he retired from the liquor trade and never recouped his vast fortune. As for the larcenous Franklin Dodge, he cajoled his way into a rewarding job with the Michigan Liquor Control Commission.[16]

Chapter 21

THE WINDSOR-DETROIT FUNNEL

With the Remus operation in disarray, John Kelly needed to repair his supply chain, so he turned his thoughts north toward the Canadian border. Canada's prohibition laws were looser than those of the US. Though liquor sales were banned, the manufacture and export of Canadian liquor were still allowed in some provinces, and enough booze had already been stockpiled near the Canada–US border to keep authorities busy for a year.

Ontario was one province that permitted liquor distilling and export. In the early 1920s, more liquor was flowing from Windsor, Ontario, through Detroit than through any other US border city. So many distillers had set up shop across the Detroit River that the crossing earned its own name, the Windsor–Detroit Funnel.

Consequently, John headed to Canada. When he drove into Detroit, one of the first sights he saw was a Ford truck half tipped over and sunk to its axles in the middle of the frozen Detroit River. The night before, a foolhardy smuggler had loaded the truck with too much weight to cross the ice. John soon learned that this type of accident happened often.

As usual when he was in a new place, John visited several speakeasies and started friendly conversations to glean the local news. Speakeasies were not hard to find. Detroit had them by the thousands, and many were controlled by a group called the Purples, who'd formed an alliance with Al Capone to transport Canadian liquor to his Outfit gang in Chicago.

Detroit had no bridges, and the ferry service was closed for the season, so John walked across the ice to Windsor. Sharp winds whistled past his ears, and he jogged to keep warm. When he passed the sunken truck, he stopped and looked back over his shoulder. Then he stomped the ringing ice, calculated the distance, and weighed the risk. He still had other sources. Cleo Lythgoe, for instance. Her warehouse in Nassau was always full. Yet every day, the police made more arrests, and John sensed that every source was as tenuous as the ice below his feet. No, he couldn't pass up a chance to tap directly into Canada.

On the Canadian side, crude wooden docks lined the riverbank, and John examined them with a curious eye. Then he asked for the way to Windsor's best distillery, where he finally met the family he'd heard about for so long, the Bronfmans, future owners of Seagram. Their Windsor-based Distillers Corporation Limited shipped a lot of liquor across Lake Erie, he had heard.

Samuel Bronfman, the family patriarch, had grown rich by exploiting the same "medicinal liquor" loophole in Canada's law that George Remus had found in the Volstead Act. The Bronfmans' "Dandy Bracer" liver and kidney cure contained sugar, molasses, tobacco, and 36 percent alcohol, and the number of their "prescriptions" equated to hundreds of thousands of gallons each year.

After the Volstead Act had passed in the US, the Bronfmans had begun to buy top-quality US distilleries, one of which was the Green Brier Distillery near Nashville. Sam Bronfman actually traveled there on his honeymoon to purchase the complete contents. Ironically, John might soon be importing whiskey made in the Green Brier Distillery—which he'd also poured in his saloon a decade earlier.

By necessity, John always carried a large roll of cash when he traveled, so after tasting Bronfman's whiskey and judging it to be genuine, he struck a bargain. The office manager wrote export forms indicating John's cargo was bound for Cuba. Then some men from the warehouse loaded John's crates onto a Ford truck, drove to the riverbank, and waited for dark.

At dusk, John stood on the bank and watched the men transfer his goods into a boat mounted on skis. An hour after dark, the riverbank came alive with trucks towing their boat-sleds onto the ice. Even with no headlights, the ragtag caravan stood out clearly on the frozen white river. Apparently, the police had been compensated not to notice. When the Bronfman truck driver towed John's boat-sled out, John followed on foot.

By starlight, the river looked as smooth as a concrete road, yet the sleds inched along at a snail's pace. Beneath their skis, the ice boomed as if it might crack, and John realized the surface was not flat at all. His crates of liquor were jolted over a moraine of frozen ridges, fissures, and overlapping shelves. The truck engine groaned and the suspension creaked. Despite the cold, John began to sweat.

He squinted through the darkness. Shadowy forms emerged from the gloom as dozens of other trucks, cars, and boat-sleds bumped across the river around him. With so much weight, could the ice hold? More than once, he saw vehicles sink into the frozen ruts and have to be pushed out by hand. An overloaded sled broke right through and disappeared with a splash, leaving a gaping hole. The other vehicles simply skirted around the hole and continued across.

Twice his own sled had to be diverted around tumbled piles of ice, and once he stopped to help another driver push his vehicle out from a crevice. At last, the Bronfman driver pulled his sled up the frozen bank into Michigan and set the brake. John climbed up on foot and wiped the sweat from his cold brow. They'd made it.

Driving his load back to Nashville, John worked things out in his mind. Before he could send his own drivers across that treacherous river, his mechanics would have to lighten and reinforce his fleet of Packards and equip them with larger tires. As details took shape in his head, he smiled, thinking how delighted his friends would be to taste Green Brier whiskey once again.

Chapter 22

JOHN TAKES HIS BRIDE TO NASSAU

Nashville's winter was turning bitterly cold. So after the holidays, John and Ethel decided to go south to The Bahamas to visit Cleo Lythgoe. John had been buying Cleo's wares all along, using various rumrunners to deliver his cargo to Florida. Cleo had often invited him to come see her again, and when she heard he was married, she renewed the invitation. It was Ethel's idea to say *yes* because, now that she'd married John, everything about his trade excited her curiosity. Naturally, she wanted to meet the famous Bahama Queen.

So at the beginning of 1925, they caught the *Dixie Flyer* train to Miami, then took an Aeromarine passenger plane to balmy Nassau. The island had undergone a transformation since John's last visit. Nassau streets were jammed full of brand-new luxury cars, and the neighborhood behind Bay Street boasted many new mansions and gardens. To John's dismay, Nassau's charming old Colonial Hotel was gone, burned down in a fire in 1922. He took a suite at the larger, more lavish New Colonial near the shore. Set in tropical gardens overlooking the picturesque Nassau Harbor, it offered tennis courts, an eighteen-hole golf course, and a superb orchestra playing dance music each night, not to mention sailing and fishing excursions, plus an exquisite private beach.

As in former times, John met Cleo in the grand dining room, where he proudly introduced his new wife. The two ladies soon took each other's measure. They shared the same good taste and clever wit, and they both adored John. That was enough to make them friends. Ethel gave a sparkling account of their honeymoon travels, and Cleo shared stories of life in Nassau.

She'd witnessed the fire in the old wooden Colonial Hotel firsthand, so she described how the red blazes lit up the night and how quickly the fire spread to nearby buildings. In the end, fireman dynamited the hotel in hopes of blowing out the flames, and it was only thanks to luck that no lives were lost. For all the criminal greed and corruption in Nassau, Cleo said on that night, the city opened its doors and hearts to the stranded visitors.

Bahamians could afford to be generous, she said, because so many of them had grown rich in the liquor trade. Even the government's coffers were overflowing. Nassau now had electric street lights, good telephone service, new roads, and a modern public water supply.

As for her business, she said she was setting new records. Every day, more American vessels were switching to British registry, and more traders were snapping up her goods. But the Coast Guard was cracking down hard on the rumrunners, and pirates were just as bad. She couldn't even guess what fraction of the liquor she sold actually made it to the US intact. The worst of it was, American crime groups were moving into Nassau.

When John heard that, he sighed. Wherever he found plentiful sources of liquor these days, he also found criminals. They were souring the business for "honest lawbreakers" like himself, and he was sad to hear they'd invaded Nassau too.

Cleo then announced that she'd met Al Capone in person. His mistress, Polly Leach, owned a house up the hill from the New Colonial, Graycliff, alleged to be the former home of Graybeard the pirate. Capone sometimes hosted parties there for his friends, and Cleo had attended one evening, just to get a look at the notorious boss. When Ethel asked what he looked like, Cleo described him as short, chubby, and hot-tempered.

After a splendid dinner, Cleo had the waiter bring out a series of liqueurs so John and Ethel could sample her newest imports. Ethel was so taken with the ornate crystal liqueur bottles that Cleo presented them to her on the spot as a wedding gift.

When their Nassau visit ended, Ethel parted from Cleo with affectionate kisses, promising to come again soon. But that promise could not be fulfilled because, later that year, 1925, Cleo was arrested. Undercover US agents seized her in Nassau and transported her to federal court in New Orleans, where she was charged with smuggling a thousand cases of whiskey into Louisiana.

Of course, she was innocent. Cleo was the agent of a lawful British whiskey dealer. She had never been a smuggler. It was her underhanded assistant who'd made a deal with a Cajun bootlegger to hijack a shipment of liquor and steer it into the bayous. When Cleo testified against the assistant, all charges against her were dropped. After that, she left the liquor trade for good.

Leaving Nassau behind, Cleo traveled for many years seeing old friends, including Bill McCoy. John kept in touch with her, but he never again found a reliable source of liquor in The Bahamas. His southern supply line was gone.

Chapter 23

A RIDE WITH THE CHIEF OF POLICE

By the summer of 1925, the list of Kelly and Sons "ice customers" was growing so rapidly that not only was John's supply chain stretched thin, he also feared his true business might soon be exposed. That would mean serious trouble, because support for Prohibition remained strong in Nashville. Situated at the heart of the Bible Belt, the city contained hundreds of churches, along with hundreds of fervent ministers condemning the "devil's drink." Happily for the Kellys, a large number of Nashville's police were on John's customer list, including the chief himself, J. W. Smith.

One Saturday morning late in the summer, J. W. telephoned John with some surprising news. A pair of strangers was selling bonded Green Brier whiskey at the edge of town, the same premium brand offered by Kelly and Sons. Who were these interlopers? John wanted to know. Were outside competitors encroaching on his territory? J. W. suggested that they go together and see the newcomers for themselves.

The chief gave John a ride in his shiny black Ford patrol car, and they drove west out Harding Pike to a fork where the road divided into State Routes 70 and 100. In the bare gravel triangle formed inside the Y, people set up stalls on Saturdays to sell their farm produce, firewood, and homemade goods. On that day, parked at one edge of this informal market, was John's own Packard roadster, and his two sons, the irrepressible Johnny and Jimmy Kelly, were selling their father's liquor out of the trunk.

J. W. doubled over with laughter, but John was not so pleased. When his sons caught sight of him, they blushed scarlet. John didn't need to say a word. Nineteen-year-old Johnny and seventeen-year-old Jimmy immediately put away the bottles, closed the trunk, and climbed into the back seat like a couple of whipped pups. John slid behind the steering wheel and drove away in stern silence. As he was pulling out, Chief J. W. Smith was still laughing.

History doesn't record what punishment John meted out, but his sons weren't bad boys. They were fun-loving and clever in school, so John couldn't stay angry for long, especially when they were only following in their father's footsteps. Johnny had done well in his first year at Millington College. His kid brother, Jimmy, was the real live wire, always pulling pranks and making mischief. Since both boys had inherited their father's good looks, they were favorites with the girls. John wished he had more free time to spend with them, and with his young daughter, Margaret. But the demands of business kept him hopping.

His ever-widening Nashville clientele was counting on his deliveries, and by mid-decade, nearly thirty employees depended on him for their livelihood. Plus, he was still paying off his loan on the Packards. More important, he had a son in college, another son and a daughter in private school, and a young wife eager to furnish their fine new home. So once again, he went out on the road to seek new supplies.

Chapter 24

CAPONE'S CHICAGO

Of all the liquor connections John Kelly made in the mid-1920s, the richest new source was in Chicago. That city was the real hub of the inland liquor trade, thanks to its many railroads and the freighter traffic across Lake Michigan, with a direct overland route of only 280 miles to Detroit. Upward of seven thousand liquor sellers operated in Chicago, including hundreds of "blind pigs"—stores with blank fronts, unmarked doors, and peepholes. Just about every time John drove to Louisville to see the horse races, he continued north to make purchases in Chicago.

He'd heard Chicago's South Side was the place to look for the best deals, and when he first arrived, what he found was an urban maze of steel factories, meatpacking plants, tenements, and speakeasies shrouded in enough smoky stench to make any visitor gag. From the late 1800s until the time of John's first visit, Chicago had expanded from thirty thousand people to nearly three million, with Poles, Italians, Irish, Germans, Greeks, Russians, and African-Americans mixing together in a rich stew of languages and cultures.

A number of groups were vying for control of the city's liquor trade, and it seemed that every time John struck a good bargain with a dealer, some rival group would take over and inflate the prices. Crime was rising so fast that the Chicago police had to divert resources from their normal law enforcement to address conflicts among the criminal groups. "Papa" Johnny Torrio was the city's biggest liquor boss, and he was grooming a young lieutenant from Brooklyn named Al Capone. By age twenty-four, Capone had worked his way up to become Torrio's right-hand man, and when Torrio was disabled in a drive-by shooting two years later, Capone became his natural successor.

It was about this time that John had his eventful meeting with Capone in the Metropole Hotel, during which he agreed to buy all his Chicago liquor from the Outfit. After the meeting, John made an effort to learn more about the enigmatic ruler of the South Side.

Truth be told, Capone had a complex, changeable nature. In a different life, he might have been capable of great achievements. He was intelligent, analytical, perceptive—an astute entrepreneur. But his violent youth had sealed his fate as a criminal. He'd grown up in one of Brooklyn's roughest neighborhoods, where thievery was a matter of survival. At age twelve, he'd dropped out of school to run errands for Manhattan's Five Points Gang. Then at twenty, he'd moved to Chicago to work as a bouncer and strong-arm for Papa Johnny Torrio.

Torrio ran Chicago's lucrative South Side, headquartered in the suburb of Cicero, and over the years he had tried to keep the peace among Chicago's many clans, including the North Side Gang and the Sicilian Genna Brothers in Little Italy. But the peace didn't hold. When the Gennas pushed too far north, the North Siders hijacked their trucks, and that set off a five-year clash during which Papa Johnny was shot and disabled.

At only twenty-six, Capone became the high king of the Chicago South Side. In some respects, he was a public benefactor, supporting charities for the poor. But the clash among the liquor groups raged on, and by the time John Kelly met Capone at the Metropole, Chicago was racking up over five hundred murders a year, far more than New York City, which was twice its size. Capone needed bodyguards to protect him.

Whether it was Capone's shrewdness or simply the times he lived in, he oversaw a revolution in the business of crime. His South Side Outfit developed intricate accounting systems, hierarchies, and alliances among an ever-widening band of people, until Capone controlled virtually all of Chicago's speakeasies, gambling halls, brothels, breweries, and distilleries.

The Outfit earned an estimated one hundred million dollars each year under Capone ($1.4 billion in today's dollars). With such outsized profits, they could afford to pay off even the highest government authorities. Thanks to this political protection, the South Side breweries and distilleries were cash cows, and everyone wanted a share. Corruption infected all levels of politics, law enforcement, and society at large. Even Chicago police chief Charles Fitzmorris admitted, "Sixty percent of my police are in the bootleg business."[17]

In 1926, Capone threw his money behind "Big Bill" Thompson's reelection campaign for Chicago mayor. Big Bill was openly pro-liquor, once going so far as to brag, "I'm wetter than the middle of the Atlantic Ocean!"[18] It was said that Thompson's portrait hung on the wall behind Al Capone's desk. When Big Bill won, Capone began boasting that he owned City Hall. His Outfit had eliminated most of his rivals by then. But his most dangerous challenger, George "Bugs" Moran of the North Side, was still out to get him.

Chapter 25

CHRISTMAS SHOPPING

After John made his deal with Capone, he and Ethel would begin to visit Chicago regularly to go shopping—though in reality, John's unspoken mission would be to purchase liquor. On their first such trip, in December just before Christmas, John brought his two sons and his daughter because he wanted to treat them all to a family get-together. They reserved a private compartment in a Pullman coach on the L&N line all the way to Louisville, then changed to the Illinois Central to complete their journey.

Despite its criminal reputation, Chicago was a large, fine city with many upscale neighborhoods, parks, and concert halls and a first-rate shopping district where families could gather in comfort. Ethel had always loved shopping at Marshall Field's department store, which operated on the motto "The customer is always right."

The Kellys arrived on a snowy afternoon, and the city lights glowed through a mist of frosty halos. Droves of cheerful shoppers coursed through the downtown streets, bundled in coats and scarves. John hailed a cab. He'd booked a suite of rooms at the Drake Hotel on Lake Shore Drive, the first choice of Chicago's high society. After depositing their luggage, the Kellys set out to enjoy the sights.

They admired the holiday window displays and visited all the smart shops and stores, collecting numerous packages along the way. Later, they caught a cab to Grant Park to see the thirty-five-foot Chicago Christmas tree decked out in a splendor of electric lights.

John enjoyed showing them around and treating them to fine meals. That night, they dined at a fashionable speakeasy called Schaller's Pump, a favorite with politicians and sports fans. John admired the fact that Schaller's had been in the same family since 1881, and he was partial to their savory chopped sirloin. Perhaps he was already thinking how grand it would be to have a restaurant of his own.

In the morning, while Ethel and the others were sight-seeing, John slipped away and bought eighty crates of liquor from Capone's Outfit. He had some of the crates wrapped with red ribbon and bows and delivered to the Illinois Central train station, where he'd reserved an entire Pullman coach to carry them.

People boarding the train were surprised to see so many Christmas gifts going home with just one family. Ethel took it in stride, but John's sons winked at each other, enjoying the attention. John paid their porters to store the crates in the pull-down sleeping berths and, with many a nudge and tease, the Kellys settled in for their long ride home.

Many hours later, when they arrived at Nashville's Union Station, the load of gifts being carried out of their private coach raised eyebrows again, and John overheard people on the platform whispering about what a wealthy family they must be. He gazed at his wife, sons, and daughter with a shine of merriment in his eyes; he thought he was very wealthy indeed.

Chapter 26

JIMMY KELLY CHOOSES A CAREER

In 1926, Hirohito became Emperor of Japan, Francisco Franco became a brigadier general in Spain, two assassination attempts were made against Mussolini, and Hitler published the second volume of *Mein Kampf*. Back home in the US, Prohibition rolled on, and due to the pervasive sale of "rotgut," thousands of people died from alcohol poisoning, while hundreds of thousands more suffered blindness or paralysis. John Kelly's supply of safe bonded whiskey became more important than ever.

In Nashville, just about the time that radio station WSM was starting up a little country music program soon to be called the *Grand Ole Opry*, John's son Jimmy turned eighteen. Jimmy Kelly had inherited his father's laughing blue eyes and his Irish gift of gab, along with a strong will. That summer, Jimmy took a stand and announced he was not going to college. He wanted to join his father's business instead.

This secretly pleased John. Though he appreciated the value of higher education, he was proud that his high-spirited boy wanted to carry on Kelly and Sons through the next generation. Jimmy was already a strapping young man—a charming rascal, but also generous and hardworking. So John gave the boy an important assignment. He sent Jimmy on the road to Florida to buy liquor.

The dense mangrove thickets along the Florida Atlantic coast made excellent entryways for Caribbean bootleggers, and liquor was plentiful around Miami. John had taken Jimmy with him once or twice and introduced him around. Now, the boy seemed enormously thrilled to be going on his own, entrusted with so much responsibility—and with such a large roll of cash. He waved goodbye from the Packard that morning and drove off with a wide grin on his face.

A week later, when he had not returned, John felt annoyed. The boy had a devil-may-care streak, and he was always up to tomfoolery. But he was a good-hearted fellow, John reminded himself. After all, wasn't he a chip off the old block? Where was the harm if he enjoyed his road trip for a few extra days?

Meanwhile, John had other matters to attend to. On his latest swing through Chicago, he'd met a young man named Walter Jacobs who'd just sold his small auto-rental company to an investor named J. D. Hertz. The car rental business had caught on all over the country, and John wasn't the only one using rentals to transport liquor. Now the Hertz Company was setting up a network of branch rental offices coast-to-coast. This gave John an idea. He went to see Mr. Hertz and explained his U-Drive-It business, then made a deal to run the Hertz branch in Nashville.

Hertz's deep pockets would make it possible for John to double his fleet, and the well-advertised national brand would provide better cover for his drivers. So after signing the papers, John caught the express train back to Nashville and replaced his old U-Drive-It sign with a bright yellow-and-black "Hertz Driv-Ur-Self" billboard.

But still, his son had not returned from Florida.

When one week lengthened into two, John grew concerned. He called his liquor suppliers and discovered the boy had completed the purchase on the first day he'd arrived. So why wasn't he back by now? Had there been an accident? A robbery? Something worse? John set off immediately to find his son.

Florida in those days was a lawless place. Thanks to the rising incomes and popularity of car travel in the Roaring Twenties, the state experienced a huge influx of tourists looking for sun and fun, as well as easy liquor, gambling, and prostitutes. Everyone from fruit growers to the governor was in the business of tourist promotion, and even the conservative state legislature voted to liberalize horse and dog racing to entertain the new visitors.

Fort Lauderdale had become known as "Fort Liquordale," and a newspaper at the time stated, "You can buy all the whiskey you want in Miami at $5 a quart." Florida business leaders warned police not to be too strict enforcing Prohibition because tourism might suffer, and even prisoners in the Dade County Jail were secretly released at night to work in the liquor trade. As Florida's public officials grew rich on graft, some Florida cities racked up the highest per capita murder rates in the nation.[19]

The courts were outrageously corrupt. For instance, when a New York millionaire, Harry S. Black, was charged with possessing a private railroad car full of liquor, the jury personally "tested the evidence" and acquitted him in five minutes.[20]

At the state's southern tip, Dade County was a rum-runner's haven. The city of Miami sparkled with swanky restaurants and hotels, right next door to illegal casinos, brothels, and bars. Eventually, Al Capone himself would buy a home near Miami Beach to escape his Chicago rivals.

Meanwhile, the ever-more-powerful Coast Guard continued its assault on what remained of Florida's dwindling Rum Row. Tourists lazing on the white sand beaches could sometimes see Coast Guard cutters roaring through the surf in hot pursuit of superfast speedboats powered by war surplus airplane engines. John Kelly thought of these things as he rushed south to find his son.

All along the route, John kept watch from his train window, terrified that he might spot the Packard crashed against a tree and poor Jimmy lying wounded in a ditch. When he reached Miami, he gave his son's description to everyone he knew. He checked hospitals. He even checked with the police.

After three sleepless nights, he tracked Jimmy to the Flamingo Hotel on Miami Beach, where the boy had been living like a high roller, gambling on the horses at Hialeah Park. Not only that, he'd persuaded his fiancée, a pretty Nashville nurse, to join him. When his father appeared, glowering with fury, Jimmy flashed the famous Kelly smile and said, "Hi, Dad!"

For the rest of that summer, Jimmy was either confined to the house or working in the rental car office under the close supervision of his father and Uncle Ed. He wasn't allowed to drive or make telephone calls, and every cent he earned went to paying back the money he'd wasted in Florida. Furthermore, he wasn't allowed to see his sweetheart—though somehow he must have stayed in touch with her, because the pretty Nashville nurse later became his wife.

Chapter 27

FLOOD TIDE

That winter, 1926, as John and Ethel were returning by train from their annual Christmas shopping trip in Chicago, they began to notice that all the creeks and rivers were out of their banks. Lakes of water stood in the fields. It had been an unusually wet year, and as their locomotive steamed southward, the rain fell harder.

When the train puffed across the bridge into Nashville, they were shocked to see how high the Cumberland River had swollen. Downtown was flooded all the way up to Third Avenue, and businesses along Lower Broadway were swamped. John realized his ice warehouse and rental garage would be flooded, but more serious were the many low-lying homes whose rooflines were barely visible above the deluge.

When they arrived at Union Station, all the talk was about the flood. The Cumberland River stood over fifty feet high and was still rising. The rain had been falling for days, and there were no dams at that time to control or divert the flow. In the station, John learned that volunteers were needed to stack sandbags to save the Woodland Street Bridge, so after seeing to his liquor crates, he sent Ethel home in a cab and ran to help.

The rain fell for eleven days in Nashville, eventually flooding the Men's Quarter all the way up to Fifth Avenue, leaving four thousand people homeless and two hundred city blocks underwater. On New Year's Day, 1927, the Cumberland River crested at over fifty-six feet (a record to this day, even higher than the devastating flood of 2010).

But this was not a local flood. John soon learned the entire Mississippi River and most of its major tributaries were overflowing. The "Father of Waters" was breaking through levees, swamping 27,000 square miles of land and displacing over 700,000 people. Ironically, the first rescuers to arrive on the scene were local bootleggers in superfast speedboats. They saved scores of residents, but still, an estimated five hundred people died.

The floodwaters lingered for months, covering broad areas of Arkansas, as well as western Tennessee and eight other states. South of Memphis, the lower Mississippi reached a width of sixty miles. The financial losses mounted to one billion dollars (about one *trillion* dollars today)—a third of the US budget in 1927.[21] Kelly and Sons spent thousands repairing their warehouse and garage.

Yet despite these massive losses, the nation's economic bubble continued to expand. Every day in 1927, the rich were getting richer, speculating on borrowed money, profiting from corruption, and pushing up the prices of everything. Executive salaries spiked to hyperbolic levels, widening the gap between management and workers. Wall Street and the banks grew fat, and any last vestige of business ethics sank into the mire. From the start of the Roaring Twenties to the year 1927, the number of American millionaires rose from twenty-one to fifteen thousand.

Moreover, by 1927, the US was home to twice the number of bars than before Prohibition, and people were consuming more liquor per capita than ever. Unfortunately, much of the liquor they drank was tainted. A government study found that, of the nearly half-million gallons of liquor confiscated in New York in 1927, nearly all contained poisons.[22] Tennessee was also awash in rotgut, and John's search for genuine bonded whiskey had never been more difficult. Like everything else, its cost was going nowhere but up.

Chapter 28

TROUBLE IN THE WINDY CITY

About the time Charles Lindbergh was making the first nonstop solo flight across the Atlantic in his single-engine *Spirit of St. Louis*, John Kelly was driving back to Nashville after picking up a load of whiskey in Detroit. As agreed, he had bought the cargo through Capone's Outfit, and as he was passing back through South Chicago, he stopped at a gas station for a fill-up. Without warning, a band of armed thugs surrounded him in broad daylight.

When John saw their guns, a storm of questions whirled through his mind. They couldn't be working for Capone. He decided they must be part of the rival North Side Gang. Chicago's northern suburbs had never been as lucrative as Capone's South Side, and lately, the northerners had been "evening the odds" by preying on Capone's liquor deliveries from Detroit.

One of the thugs slammed John against the car and frisked him. The men took his pocket watch and his wallet full of cash, then jerked the diamond ring off his finger. They moved quickly, grunting only a few short words. Then they sped off in John's Packard, taking his liquor with them.

Left alone in the street, John shoved his hands in his pockets and sighed. Worse things had happened. At least he was still alive. He walked into the gas station and called the Metropole Hotel. "This is John Kelly," he told Capone's lieutenant. "I've just been robbed."

There was a muffled exchange, then the boss himself came on the line. Capone asked for a description of the men and the vehicle they were driving. "OK," he said, "I'll take care of it. Come to the Metropole, and we'll have a room for you."

John didn't speak to Capone again, and he couldn't guess how Capone might "take care of it." He simply hailed a cab and spent a sleepless night at the Metropole Hotel. The next morning, Capone kept his promise. John received a message with the address of a warehouse on Wabash Avenue. When he arrived there, one of Capone's men met him at the door. Inside, his Packard was waiting, unscathed and still loaded with whiskey.

"Here's your stuff," the man said, handing over John's watch, diamond ring, and wallet. "Mr. Capone says not to worry. This won't happen again, and he wishes you a safe trip home."

John didn't count the money in his wallet. He could tell by the feel that it was all still there. He thanked the man, climbed into his car, and slowly drove away, marveling that such a ruthless boss as Al Capone could also be a man of his word.

Yet John's worries weren't over. Hijackings and robberies were on the rise, and law enforcement along the US–Canada border had grown so intense that only the most foolhardy dared to cross the river at Detroit anymore. In 1928, the Bronfman family bought the Seagram Distillery from founder Joseph E. Seagram in Ontario, but like other Canadian distillers, they switched their trade routes eastward toward the Atlantic, sailing their schooners under cover of darkness.

Down along the southern coast, the once-invincible Rum Row had become a ghost of itself, due largely to the Coast Guard crackdown, but also in part to the Great Okeechobee Hurricane of 1928, the deadliest ever recorded on the Atlantic Coast. Sweeping through the Caribbean into Florida, it left thousands dead. Once again, the swift rumrunner speedboats were the first rescuers on the scene. But that didn't stop the Coast Guard patrols.

A few weeks after John was robbed in Chicago, Bugs Moran and his North Side Gang attacked Al Capone, peppering his headquarters with over a thousand rounds of machine gun fire. But Capone seemed to have miraculous luck at dodging the gunfire with the help of his bulletproof Cadillac and his ever-present army of bodyguards. Though Moran made several attempts on Capone's life, he never wounded him.

All the same, when Moran's North Side Gang continued to hijack Capone's trucks, members of Capone's Outfit planned a retaliation. Early on the morning of February 14, 1929, they entered Moran's North Side headquarters dressed as police officers in what appeared to be a raid in search of illegal whiskey, taking Moran's men by surprise.

The result was the infamous St. Valentine's Day massacre, which was reported on the front page of every newspaper in the country. Capone was away at his Florida estate and was never linked to the crime. But seven men died that day, and the North Side group never fully recovered. In Washington, President Hoover's team assigned the investigation of bootlegging to a young US Treasury agent, Eliot Ness.

Naturally, John was distressed to hear of these events. A state of war existed in the liquor trade, and all the roads were growing more dangerous. He and Ethel had just had their first child, a daughter they named Patricia. Frankly, John longed to go back to the days of being a simple saloonkeeper in Nashville, serving his customers with a hearty welcome, great food, and a generous pour of whiskey.

Often he imagined retiring from the trade and opening an elegant restaurant in Nashville—if only this Prohibition law could be repealed. He was not alone in wanting that. Even the staunchest temperance supporters were beginning to doubt the so-called noble experiment of Prohibition. The problem was, the law was still on the books. If John retired now, his dream restaurant would have no fine whiskey to serve.

Chapter 29

THE CRASH

By the end of the 1920s, the stock market had risen to giddy heights. Though many of John Kelly's friends and customers were buying shares, he kept plowing his profits back into his own enterprise, rewarding his employees, maintaining his fleet of vehicles, and buying more bonded liquor for his warehouses.

Kelly and Sons Ice Company was still going strong, thanks in large part to the liquor that accompanied most orders. Yet John could already foresee the end of the ice business. Mechanical cooling systems had been around since the Civil War, and refrigerated railcars were now commonly used to ship meats and other perishables. General Electric had been marketing a gas-powered home refrigerator for years, and in 1927 they introduced a new electric model. John knew it wouldn't be long before the ice trade disappeared.

Yet his confidence remained high, and he felt surrounded by opportunity. His hometown of Nashville had become a financial powerhouse, earning the title "Wall Street of the South." John knew just about every banker, broker, and insurance executive in the city. Many counted on Kelly and Sons for their liquor, and

John and Ethel socialized with their families. John heard their talk about the vast wealth to be made speculating in the stock market, but he preferred to trust his own endeavors. Still, he was proud of his flourishing city.

Nashville banks dominated the downtown skyline, along with brokerage firms and two rival insurance companies, National Life & Accident and Life & Casualty, both of which acquired radio stations to advertise their products. The radio call letters WLAC stood for "W-Life And Casualty." WSM, owned by National Life & Accident, took its call letters from the motto, "We Shield Millions."

Through it all, John went about his daily business of maintaining the supply chain and serving his customers. His choice not to speculate in stocks was fortunate, because that autumn, the overblown market abruptly toppled in a crash that echoed around the world. People called it Black Tuesday—October 29, 1929. In that single day, over sixteen million shares traded hands on the New York Stock Exchange, and billions of speculation dollars vanished.

Yet even the financial chaos could not deter Treasury agent Eliot Ness. He and his so-called Untouchables were raiding scores of speakeasies, distilleries, and breweries. One morning in 1930, eighteen federal agents—dressed in their trademark fedoras and trench coats—descended on John Kelly's home on Woodmont Boulevard. Apparently, someone had tipped them off about John's dealings in Chicago.

John and his family were directed to the front yard, while the agents searched their house. He wasn't worried. Though he maintained a large liquor inventory in various warehouses throughout Nashville, he never stored any at home. He was far too cautious for that.

Unfortunately, he'd forgotten about the decorative crystal liqueur bottles that Cleo Lythgoe had given his wife as a wedding gift years earlier. He and Ethel seldom drank liqueur, so the gift had slipped his mind. Yet Ethel treasured the elegant cut crystal bottles, and she had displayed them in a window where the jewel-colored liqueurs would catch the afternoon sunlight. When Ness's men saw the bottles, they pounced. Would he be arrested in front of his family? Would his children see him in handcuffs? But then he noticed something odd. The liqueur bottles were almost empty. Their ornate stoppers were tightly sealed, so he knew the liqueur couldn't have evaporated.

All at once, the family maid fled toward the kitchen, and one glance at her cringing expression gave John a clue. With a quiet laugh, he demanded that the agents measure the liqueur. The liquor law allowed private citizens to keep a small amount of spirits in their homes. When the agents found the remaining liqueur was within the legal limit, they stomped to their caravan of automobiles and sped away down Woodmont Boulevard. The famous Untouchables had no choice but to let Nashville's most illustrious liquor trader go free.

Then John went to the kitchen to look for the maid. The woman was hiding in the pantry, and when he approached, she tried to stammer an apology. As he had guessed, she'd been sneaking little nips for years.

"Never mind," he said, silencing her with a grin. "You've saved me a lot of trouble." To show his thanks, he took a fifty-dollar bill from his wallet and slipped it into her trembling hand.

Chapter 30

REPEAL AT LAST

Late in 1930, the steep economic decline that had already overtaken other parts of the country moved into Nashville. Some say the dominoes began to fall on November 7, 1930, when examiners audited the Bank of Tennessee and declared it insolvent. The bank was owned by Caldwell & Company, a bond brokerage run by James Caldwell's son, Rogers, referred to by the press as "J. P. Morgan of the South."

When the bank failed, Caldwell & Company went bankrupt. Because of its relationships with so many other banks, its collapse led to nearly one hundred additional bank failures across the South. Among the many financial shortfalls, the Tennessee state treasury lost over six million dollars on its bond investments (about seventy-two million in today's dollars).

Indeed, the bad times were just beginning for Nashville. Businesses began to lay off workers, and many businesses closed down. Soon breadlines and soup kitchens sprang up all over the city. John felt thankful to be able to keep his people employed. His business didn't fall off during that stressful time. If anything, his dejected customers needed a lift of "spirits" more than ever.

Then in 1932, not long after Al Capone was sentenced to eleven years in prison for tax evasion, federal agents in Nashville finally discovered one of John's liquor warehouses and pulled a surprise raid. When John got the telephone call, he had an immediate suspicion who the informers were. He leased the warehouse from a moving and storage company, and he'd suspected for years that the owner's two sons were stealing his liquor. He guessed the boys had called in the feds to cover up their theft.

Sure enough, the reported volume of liquor seized and destroyed by the agents that day was considerably less than what John had accounted for on his inventory sheet. Luckily, the agents couldn't prove who owned the liquor because the warehouse was rented through a fictitious name. Consequently, no charges were filed. John's suspicions about the boys were later confirmed when they disappeared from Nashville.

The year 1933 brought a pivotal moment in history. Franklin D. Roosevelt was inaugurated as the US president, and far away in Europe, Hitler became chancellor of Germany. However, the two events that most affected John Kelly that year were the birth of his youngest son, my father, Bill, and the repeal of Prohibition.

In December 1933, Utah cast the final vote needed to ratify the Twenty-First Amendment, thereby repealing a law that had brought the nation to the brink of chaos. The Twenty-First Amendment was the only one in US history to reverse another amendment and the only one ratified by state conventions rather than state legislatures.

Though Tennessee's convention voted to repeal Prohibition, Tennessee's state legislature did not repeal the state's dry laws. Thus, Tennessee continued to ban all liquor sales within its borders for the next six years. In Nashville, however, Mayor Hilary Howse was still in office, and the local liquor trade continued its business as usual. So Kelly and Sons Ice Company kept making the rounds.

Once again that Christmas, John took his family to Chicago for a "shopping trip." On the return journey in their private Pullman coach, his youngest two children slept on mattresses covering the crates of liquor in the pull-down berths. John hoped this might be the last such trip. With Prohibition repealed, he felt certain that other states would be quick to make liquor legal again, so there would be no more need to smuggle cargo on trains or hide deliveries in ice trucks.

He foresaw his chance to serve customers in a brand-new way. He would open a real dinner club.

PART III

SPEAKEASIES

John Kelly in downtown Nashville

The Kelly family is celebrating Christmas at the 216 Club.

John and Ethel Kelly at the 216 Club

A Kelly family dinner at the 216 Club

A WSM crew at the 216 Club

A matchbook cover from the 216 Dinner Club

Bill Kelly serving as a bartender pouring drinks at the 216 Dinner Club.

Bill Kelly with the notorious Friday Night Group

Jimmy Kelly's on Harding Road

Jimmy Kelly, Bill Kelly, and Johnny Grubbs are behind the bar at the Harding Road location.

Jimmy Kelly and his wife, Thelma

Jimmy Kelly's Steakhouse

Mike Kelly welcoming guests at the Louise Avenue location

William “Buster” Ramson, head waiter, always had a smile.

Arthur White behind the bar entertaining guests

Willie Fisher, Fred Lee, Carl Worthy, Robert Olden, and "Little Joe" Overton

Tinker Kelly, Ray Bell, Bill Kelly, and Mike Kelly

Bruce Dobie, Tom Ingram, John J. Hooker, and Mike Kelly in deep discussion at the "power table."

Bill Yeaman and Susan DePriest are enjoying dinner in the main dining room.

The Grand Staircase

Lee Parrish, Bar Manager

Fred Lee

View of the patio

View of the main dining room

Chapter 31

THE PERFECT LOCATION

In former times, John Kelly had taken pleasure in welcoming people to his saloon. Now, as he planned his new restaurant, he made a pledge to himself and his future customers. He would serve a juicy, well-aged steak and a generous pour of whiskey with service that was always welcoming and attentive. He felt sure that making good on that pledge would guarantee his success as a restaurateur.

Then, as now, a restaurant's location was pivotal, so John's first task was to find the ideal site. He wanted to situate his club at the heart of Nashville's commercial and entertainment life. In 1934, even in the throes of the Great Depression, that vibrant heart was downtown. He looked for a spot on Cedar Street, near where his former saloon had stood, but what he found was even closer to the action on Cedar Knob (known today as Capitol Hill).

For years, the state capitol building had hummed with legislators, lawyers, and lobbyists—a hungry and thirsty bunch indeed. John's chosen site was just one block south of the capitol building, near Union Street with its cluster of banks and financial companies—whose executives also liked to eat and drink. A block farther south was Church Street, the city's main shopping district, anchored by two Nashville department store chains, Castner Knott and Cain–Sloan. These and other shops drew families from all over Middle Tennessee.

John's spot also lay in sight of many upscale hotels for traveling businessmen and visitors. The historic Maxwell House had hosted seven US presidents. The Hermitage was Nashville's first million-dollar hotel, and the massive Andrew Jackson Hotel boasted four hundred guest rooms. Closest of all would be the elegant Hotel Tulane, where twenty-five years earlier Colonel Cooper had planned his shoot-out with Senator Edward Carmack. In fact, the Tulane would be right next door.

Just across the street from John's club stood two singular destinations. The WSM radio station drew musicians from all over the South to perform on its live broadcasts, and the War Memorial Auditorium hosted world-famous theatrical events, opera singers, and traveling shows. Not far away, the Ryman Auditorium had long been welcoming such performers as Sarah Bernhardt, the Metropolitan Opera, and the Imperial Russian Ballet, not to mention hosting championship boxing matches.

To the north lay the Sulphur Dell baseball field, home to the Nashville Volunteers, a Class A baseball club that was hugely popular in Middle Tennessee. Downtown was abuzz on game nights, and many baseball fans stopped by for food, drinks, and a bit of sports talk both before and after the games.

Elegant movie theatres were clustered around John's new location as well, including the Vendome, a palace of marble floors, balconies, and deep red upholstery. Nearby stood Tony Sudekum's Princess Theatre, the Knickerbocker, and the Elite. The 1930s were Hollywood's Golden Age, producing films such as *Gone with the*

Wind and *The Wizard of Oz*. Going to the movies in those days was an event that almost always involved dinner at a restaurant.

John had grown up on these downtown streets. As he walked along gazing at the passersby, he knew he'd found his niche. He would provide a comfortable dining alternative to the city's more formal hotels, plus a respectable drinking alternative to the rowdy downtown speakeasies. His restaurant would be a place where men could bring their ladies. Not only would he welcome people drawn to the city's night life, he would also provide Nashville's first real business lunch spot, where lawmakers and executives could discuss matters in comfort.

After long and careful thought, he signed the lease for the pleasant, two-story residence next door to the Hotel Tulane. The street address was 216 Eighth Avenue North. Following the example of the 21 Club in New York, he named his establishment by its street number. In 1934, John Kelly's 216 Dinner Club opened its doors for business.

Chapter 32

THE 216 CLUB'S EARLY BEGINNINGS

John made several wise decisions when he opened the 216 Club. First and foremost, he continued his tradition of serving only the finest bonded liquors, which he purchased from trusted sources in nearby states. And second, he made a credo of the generous pour.

Since both the manufacture and sale of spirits were still illegal in Tennessee, he followed the true speakeasy tradition of installing a peephole beside his locked entrance in order to get a good look at anyone who came knocking. He kept only a small liquor inventory on the premises, and his bartenders served the drinks from porcelain pitchers, color-coded red for bourbon, yellow for scotch, and blue for gin. In case of a police raid, the doorman would sound a buzzer to alert everyone, and bartenders would quickly dump the open pitchers down the sink.

This would later prove expedient because, although liquor enforcement under Mayor Howse was lax, the city police did stage the occasional raid. In the case of the 216 Club, where many politicians and police officers were customers, they would usually call ahead as a courtesy. John would pay a minor fine, the case would be dropped, and the mayor would probably dine there that evening.

John bought a long, ornate bar hand-carved in Germany from a single piece of black walnut. To further enrich the club's ambiance, he asked a family friend, Micky Strobel, to paint murals on the walls in the upstairs dining room. According to legend, Strobel took his pay for that job in whiskey.

The plucky Strobel had a reputation around town for his eye-catching artwork. He'd started out as a carnival snake trainer, graduated to prizefighting, then landed as a staff artist at the *Nashville Tennessean*. Eventually he moved to Chicago, where he earned fame and fortune as a celebrated illustrator and as art director for *Playboy* magazine. The stunning murals he created for the 216 Club had an air of the Arabian Nights: on a black background were swaying palm trees, galloping horses, and larger-than-life voluptuous harem girls. Mystical genies danced about the walls, which added to the club's beguiling aura.

In another smart move, John hired the head chef from the Maxwell House Hotel, who brought along his mother's secret recipe for corn cakes. These buttery, mouthwatering treats were the size of silver dollars, and they became a standout hit with diners. John's kitchen also served up a salad originally created by his good friend Xavier Faucon, a French chef who'd owned Faucon's Café, located on Union Street, before he'd returned home to Louisiana eight years previously. The Faucon salad is a mix of salty bacon, hard-boiled eggs, and bleu cheese served over a bed of chilled, chopped iceberg lettuce. John's son, Jimmy Kelly, would later add both these items to his own restaurant menu, where they remain Nashville favorites.

John believed in close-knit families, and like his father before him, he hired his relatives. His son Jimmy took to the business like a bird to the air. Jimmy worked every job in the club at one time or another, and he developed a knack for striking good bargains and saving money. At twenty-six, he was married to the pretty nurse, Thelma, and he'd grown into a perfect gentleman. He was still fond of pranks and good times, but he was charming and gallant, always immaculate in a tailored suit and tie, and growing more savvy by the day about the restaurant trade.

John also hired his son-in-law, Bob Woolwine, who proved to be an able, levelheaded manager of the restaurant's day-to-day operations and staff. John understood the importance of staff. He wanted his customers to feel he was personally welcoming them into his home for drinks and dinner, and he knew from experience that a happy staff was essential. So he made a point of hiring the right people, treating them well, and rewarding their success. He showed sincere respect for everyone, from porters and kitchen help to drivers and bartenders.

As a result, his employees took pride in their work and stayed loyal over time, learning not only to greet the customers by name, but also to remember their favorite tables, drinks, menu items, and birthdays. This gracious personal attention set the 216 Club apart from all others, and the customers returned again and again.

Chapter 33

HUEY LONG VISITS NASHVILLE

Just a few weeks after opening, John welcomed the first of a long list of big celebrities to the 216 Club, and one of the biggest was "the Kingfish," Huey Long. On October 27, 1934, Long brought five thousand LSU football fans to Nashville on a chartered train to see the LSU Tigers play against Vanderbilt.

As a former Louisiana governor and current US senator, Long was a controversial but much-loved American figure. He had an outsized personality and a large populist following, and thousands met his train at Union Station, including the ever-colorful Mayor Hilary Howse. Many hoped Long would announce his run for US president, and the cheering crowds followed his marching band through downtown in what was probably Nashville's largest parade since the homecoming welcome for Sergeant Alvin York, the Tennessee hero of World War I.

People packed War Memorial Auditorium to hear Long's address, but instead of announcing his candidacy, he won his audience with compliments. Ever the consummate politician, he paid tribute to Andrew Jackson for rescuing Louisiana at the Battle of New Orleans, and he claimed that Vanderbilt was his second favorite football team, after LSU.

When Long finished his address, Mayor Howse escorted him and his coterie of bodyguards, newspaper reporters, and anyone else who could squeeze into the 216 Club for refreshments. John Kelly met them at the door and joined them at their table, where the talk quickly turned to football. John and the mayor were both avid Vanderbilt fans, and Long had a passion for the LSU Tigers, so along with their drinks, the men shared plenty of cordial boasting and ribbing.

Long enjoyed himself thoroughly. Before he left, he praised the quality of the 216 Club and promised to come every time he visited Nashville.

Visits from celebrities such as Huey Long helped put the 216 Club on the map. Tragically, before a year had passed, Huey Long was assassinated.

Chapter 34

THE CLUB'S GROWING SUCCESS

John Kelly's sixty-five-cent lunch proved popular with downtown lawmakers, businessmen, shopgirls, and secretaries alike. In those days, ordering drinks with lunch was commonplace, and so was having a few drinks with colleagues after work. Various organizations held luncheon and dinner meetings there. Moreover, since the building had once been a residence, a number of small private rooms opened off the main "front parlor," and the club soon became the place where deals were made.

John's longtime friend, attorney John Hooker Sr., had a regular table, and when his Belle Meade house burned and his family moved into the Hermitage Hotel, they took their lunches and dinners at John's club every day. In fact, many families felt comfortable taking meals in the 216 Club (excluding minors, of course). Since lavish homes were smaller in those days, when people entertained, they often hosted their parties at the 216 Club. It offered one of the few bars in Nashville where ladies felt at ease.

The wealthy Coca-Cola distributor, Julius B. Weil, once said the 216 Club was the only speakeasy where he would permit gentlemen callers to take his daughter Peggy (later Peggy Steine) because he trusted John and Jimmy to watch over her. When Peggy's date got drunk at dinner one night, Jimmy came to her rescue. He alerted Peggy's father, then called a cab to take her home. These stories were often told by Peggy over dinner at the restaurant.

Staff members at the 216 Club were always doing special favors. My uncle, Bob Woolwine, once lent his car to an out-of-towner who'd missed his train and needed a way to get home. That was the kind of hospitality people came to expect at John Kelly's place. Nashvillians knew that when they came there, they would be among friends.

In time, a group of businessmen began to meet there every Friday night. They were lovers of good conversation, and they called themselves "the Friday Night Club." They discussed everything from the latest business trends to the arts, literature, politics, and science. They even plotted advertising campaigns. And they enjoyed practical jokes.

Once, when a group member was out of town and couldn't attend, he sent a live goat by express train, along with a letter introducing the goat as his stand-in for the evening. The Friday Night Club took it in stride and welcomed the goat to their meeting, placing his front hooves on the bar and taking his photograph for posterity. Unfortunately, there's no record of the goat's remarks during the evening's discussion.

Chapter 35

TENNESSEE LIQUOR LAWS BEGIN TO LOOSEN

The Great Depression of the 1930s was the longest and deepest economic decline of the century, afflicting people and nations around the world. In Tennessee, the effects were felt from the farmlands to the inner cities. Yet the hardships of that decade inspired many new ideas and progressive solutions. Thanks to support from Nashville mayor Hilary Howse, Hill McAlister won two terms as governor, bringing New Deal dollars and jobs to Tennessee. Mayor Howse himself obtained federal WPA funds to complete the Nashville Courthouse and Berry Field Airport in 1936. From John Kelly's point of view, 1936 brought another huge win because Lem Motlow gained a seat in the Tennessee state legislature.

Motlow's primary reason for entering politics was to once again make legal the making of whiskey in Tennessee. He felt sure it would be a boon to the local economy, but his most earnest desire was to reestablish his uncle Jack Daniel's distillery near the pure spring waters and rich cornfields of Lynchburg. Of course, John Kelly was as eager to see that happen as anyone.

Rains fell heavily that winter of 1936 when a region-wide weather system set up over the Tennessee, Ohio, and Mississippi river basins, leading to another disastrous flood, worse even than the calamity of 1927. In January 1937, high water inundated thousands of square miles and left a million people homeless. It was said that a person could travel by boat from Tuscaloosa, Alabama, to El Paso, Texas, a distance of more than twelve hundred miles.

Nashville was hit especially hard when the Cumberland River crested at a new record high (again, higher than Nashville's 2010 flood). The US Army Corps of Engineers was charged with flood control on the Cumberland, but many of its dams and reservoirs were still in the planning stage. Likewise, the Tennessee Valley Authority had been in operation less than four years and had not yet completed its flood control plans. Nashville's Sulphur Dell baseball field was swamped, as well as hundreds of low-lying homes and businesses.

John no longer kept warehouses along the riverbank, so he suffered no material damage. But many friends and neighbors did, so like most Nashvillians, John and his sons volunteered for the rescue effort. Mayor Howse deployed every city vehicle to evacuate the hardest-hit areas in East Nashville, and he worked tirelessly through the crisis to rescue and shelter the citizenry. Waters rose so high that, in a controversial move, the Corps of Engineers dynamited levees, flooding farmlands to save population centers. All told, the flood caused damages in the hundreds of millions of dollars (what would be billions today), and it prompted passage of the US Flood Control Act of 1936.

Nashville was still recuperating from the flood when Nashville's beloved Mayor Howse died in office. Howse had been a good friend to John Kelly, and during his reign, Nashville drinking establishments had operated virtually trouble free,with little interference from law enforcement. Most citizens seemed to like it that way, and traveling businessmen were pleased that Nashville offered sociable places to meet associates for drinks.

Because fashionable bars and restaurants such as the 216 Club and the hotels supported the local economy, most Nashvillians were glad to see Howse succeeded by Vice Mayor Thomas L. Cummings Sr., future founder of Cummings Sign and another opponent of the liquor ban. Cummings, too, was John's good friend and customer. (Years later when Cummings's son, Tom, came home on leave from the army, Cummings brought the young man to Jimmy Kelly's to celebrate his twenty-first birthday with his first legal drink.)

Despite the flood and the loss of Mayor Howse, Lem Motlow was able to shepherd his distillery legalization act through the state legislature later that year. The act limited distilleries to only three counties: Lincoln, Coffee, and Lem's own Moore County. This reduced competition and gave Jack Daniel's Distillery a chance to rebuild and thrive at Cave Spring Hollow in Lynchburg.

Though Prohibition was over, the nation was still awash in bad-tasting whiskey, mostly labeled as bourbon. When Lem Motlow started making whiskey again, the smartest thing he did was to take the word *bourbon* off his label to differentiate his product from the cheap liquor sold everywhere at the time. This required lengthy discussions with Washington officials over labeling requirements. In the end, they agreed that if Lem filtered out at least 2 percent of the solids in his whiskey, he could differentiate it enough to avoid including *bourbon* in the name.

Lem hired laborers to harvest some of the abundant sugar maple saplings that grew around Lynchburg, then burn them down to charcoal in earthen pits. He used this charcoal to filter his whiskey, resulting in the distinctively mellow flavor that's now so much admired. Satisfied with the taste, he created a new name, "Tennessee Sipping Whiskey," and the Jack Daniel's brand was on its way to worldwide fame.

Over seventy years would pass before Tennessee expanded its law to permit distilleries in other counties. But in 1939, the state legislature handed John and his friends another windfall by permitting the sale of "liquor by the bottle" as a county option. Though serving drinks "by the ounce" was still banned statewide, the law authorized individual counties to decide whether to allow packaged liquor stores. Nashville's Davidson County voted a resounding *yes*, and since citizens were now free to purchase bottles, many interpreted the law to mean they could also bring their bottles to restaurants to share with friends.

Hence, Nashville speakeasies began to reinvent themselves as private bottle clubs, and the 216 Club was one of the first to convert.

Chapter 36

THE 216 CLUB BECOMES FAMOUS

Immediately after "liquor by the bottle" was legalized in Nashville in 1939, John Kelly did two things to make his 216 Club appear more legitimate. First, he displayed shelves of bottles ostensibly owned by private individuals and labeled with their names. Second, he established his own 215 Liquor Store in the small annex building behind his club.

Some customers did bring their own bottles to keep on John's shelves, and some did buy packaged liquor from his store. But in the main, John's new system was a ruse. Though the names on the bottles were real, the liquor was available for sale to everyone. And the package store was really just a safe, convenient stockroom for the club's inventory.

Nashville officialdom generally gave this system a nod of acceptance, and many other private bottle clubs sprang up in and around Nashville, though few of the names are still remembered: Nero's, Carousel, Wagon Wheel, Doc Manion's Pines, Celtic Lounge, and Hettie Ray's. Some charged a fifty-cent admission, some offered music or gambling, and most offered some type of food. They all displayed bottles labeled with customers' names, and they all served liquor freely to anyone who ordered. Some bars sold locker keys with each bottle, and these so-called locker clubs were just another form of the same widely accepted ruse.

By 1940, the 216 Club was *the* place where everyone met, and business was so good that John introduced a valet parking service, handing out numbered brass coins as receipts. Not only did the Nashville elite hobnob at John's club but so did the many traveling salesmen, executives, and a growing number of military personnel. The United States, neutral at the time, had been uneasily watching events develop in both Europe and Asia-Pacific, while preparing for the inevitable. Since Nashville was central to half the US population, it was a hub of activity.

General George S. Patton chose the Middle Tennessee countryside to practice tank and infantry maneuvers because the terrain resembled that of Western Europe, and hundreds of thousands of soldiers went through training not far from Nashville. The area's army bases included Camp Campbell in Clarksville, Camp Forrest in Tullahoma, and Camp Tyson in Paris, Tennessee.

When camp commanders issued weekend passes, the soldiers rushed toward Nashville, just as they had in previous wars, because Nashville was the nearest city where a man could get a fine meal, a decent drink, and a night of rewarding entertainment. Many commanders recommended the 216 Club by name, knowing their young men would be well looked after. When soldiers were in town, their revels were so loud that every night at the 216 Club felt like New Year's Eve.

On December 7, 1941, following the attack on Pearl Harbor, the US entered the war, and rationing was one of the many changes this brought to the home front in 1942. Once again, beef, sugar, grain, and other foods were restricted, and liquor production was sharply curtailed due to the military's need for alcohol.

But thanks to John's arrangement two decades earlier between Lem Motlow and John Hooker Sr., the 216 Club had access to an ample supply of Jack Daniel's rare prewar whiskey. Mr. Hooker kept an inventory in his basement, and just about every day, Jimmy drove to his house to load up more crates. Nashville insiders knew that Captain Jack's strong, smooth Old No. 7 whiskey always flowed at the 216 Club.

Several times during the war years, police raided the restaurant but always with the courtesy of an advance warning. John Kelly persuaded a friend on the police force to cite the restaurant for having more than their wartime allotment of whiskey and beef. He paid his fine of $25 as usual, but frugal as always, John and young Jimmy saw the police raids as an opportunity for free advertising. The news would make the front page of both newspapers, and for the next few weeks the club's dinner trade would skyrocket.

Musicians, songwriters, and music promoters made up another big share of John's clientele. The Grand Ole Opry had become a national hit, and in the early 1940s, WSM radio began to broadcast the show before a live audience in the War Memorial Auditorium, a few steps from John's front door. The show drew fans, performers, and crew from all over the South, and many of them dropped into the 216 Club for refreshments before, during, and after the broadcast. Some of the WSM crew even made a prank photo album for John as a joke.

Since the club stayed open till dawn, many were the nights when musicians launched into informal jam sessions. Roy Acuff, Bill Monroe, Gene Autry, and Roy Rogers were among the numerous top entertainers to enjoy John's generous pour. When the Opry moved a few blocks away to the Ryman Auditorium in 1943, the music people still returned. They said the 216 Club felt like home.

Another familiar face at John's club was the Ryman's manager, a quirky, eccentric woman named Lula Naff. She went by her initials, L. C. Naff, to avoid gender bias in the male-dominated entertainment business, and she was a tough, diligent promoter, battling Nashville censorship groups in order to book world-famous entertainers. It was through her work that the Ryman became known as the "Carnegie Hall of the South." L. C. brought in such acts as Harry Houdini, Bob Hope, Charlie Chaplin, W. C. Fields, and others, many of whom she treated to drinks and dinner at the 216 Club.

Sports celebrities also found their way to John's door, often escorted by Fred Russell, a nationally known sportswriter and long-time Nashvillian. Russell authored books and wrote for popular national magazines such the *Saturday Evening Post*, as well as serving as sports editor and columnist at the *Nashville Banner*. Like Jimmy Kelly, Russell was fond of a good joke and was always ready to laugh, even at himself. He knew all the top sports figures, from jockeys and ball-players to championship boxers, and everybody loved him.

Grantland Rice and Bobby Jones were both regulars at the club. Vandy graduate Rice covered sports for the *New York Tribune* and Paramount Pictures newsreels, while legendary golfer Jones cofounded and codesigned the world-renowned Augusta National Golf Club, two hours east of Atlanta, Georgia. Both men hung out at John's bar whenever they were in town, regaling the crowd with sports stories.

By the time World War II ended on September 2, 1945, the Great Depression was over, and Nashville was awash in optimism. Entrepreneurs were launching new ventures, and the city's many colleges and universities were thriving. Its four medical schools were laying the foundations for what would soon become Nashville's most vital economic engine: the health-care industry.

Moreover, the hugely successful Grand Ole Opry was drawing first-rate musicians from across the US and beyond. It was only natural for the recording industry to follow.

In 1948, Nashville's first music recording studio began operating directly next door to the 216 Club. Starting on a shoestring budget, Castle Studios converted a dining room in the Hotel Tulane to accommodate their sound equipment. One of their first successes was a Tin Pan Alley tune performed by a young singer-songwriter named Hank Williams. "Lovesick Blues" topped the country charts for sixteen weeks in 1949 and crossed over into the Top 25 pop charts as well. In short order, Williams and Castle Studios soared into the national spotlight. And all of them, from the sound mixer to the singer himself, hung their hats at the 216 Club.

Out-of-town performers stayed at the Hotel Tulane during their Castle recording sessions, and most took their meals at John's club. After late-night sessions, the club was a handy place to relax, strum a few tunes, and write new songs. For Hank Williams, it was a favorite place to drink.

Williams had a brilliant musical gift, but he was a wild young man with reckless habits that often brought him trouble. One late night at the Tulane, he set his hotel room on fire while smoking in bed. People in the 216 Club saw the flames through the window and called the fire department. Hank was arrested on a misdemeanor charge of smoking in a hotel room—he also singed his hair and beard—and had to endure the teasing of his buddies at the 216 Club. Sadly, alcohol would ultimately be Hank's undoing at age twenty-nine.

Those raucous old times were wonderful, but nothing lasts forever. Jack Daniel's proprietor Lem Motlow had died in late 1947 and the distillery passed to his heirs. Then, at the age of sixty-five, while resting in his home and attended by his beloved Ethel, John Kelly also passed away in 1948.

Kelly's life spanned one of America's most volatile periods. He'd witnessed the advent of the automobile and commercial flight, Prohibition, the Roaring Twenties, the stock market crash, the Great Depression, and two world wars. But now a new era was beginning. The postwar years were ushering in one of the longest economic booms the world had ever seen, and Nashville was rapidly changing. Affluent residents were leaving downtown and moving out to the suburbs, where new shopping centers and movie theatres were sprouting up overnight. Under the steadfast management of Bob Woolwine, the 216 Club continued to thrive at its downtown location for another seventeen years.

But young Jimmy Kelly decided to strike out on his own. One year after his father's death, he opened Jimmy Kelly's in Nashville's most prestigious suburb, Belle Meade.

PART IV

NASHVILLE'S OLDEST FINE DINING RESTAURANT

Chapter 37

JIMMY KELLY'S MOVE TO BELLE MEADE

Belle Meade takes its name from the antebellum plantation of the same name, once the site of John Harding's famous Thoroughbred stud farm. In the early 1900s, the plantation was sold to the Belle Meade Land Company, and developer John Bransford laid it out as a residential subdivision. While the streets were being built, one of the owners—a Tennessee newspaper magnate and former US senator named Luke Lea—donated 267 acres at the heart of the property to be developed as a world-class golf club. Bransford, Lea, and the other influential owners exerted their considerable clout to ensure that a Nashville streetcar line would be extended to the property.

Nashville's elite soon took up residence in Belle Meade. In 1916, the stately new Nashville Golf and Country Club began hosting Nashville's most exclusive social events, welcoming such luminaries as Bing Crosby and Billy Graham, while its equally important sports tournaments were attracting big-name golfers such as Sam Snead. Later, the tony, three-square-mile neighborhood of Belle

Meade became an independent city through incorporation, and in 1921 the directors of the golf club changed its name to Belle Meade Country Club. An enclave for the affluent, Belle Meade was a place where refined, lush-lawned mansions were hewed just to the cusp of understatement. More importantly, it was a place where new money could grow "old," fast. Savvy entrepreneur that he was, Jimmy Kelly would locate his new dinner club there in 1949. He wanted to be close to the leading families' natural comfort zone, while continuing to burnish his reputation as their preferred purveyor of nourishment and libations.

Jimmy was ahead of the curve in making the leap to the suburbs, as most of the other private bottle clubs remained downtown. With the Harding Road site he chose directly across from the popular Belle Meade movie theatre, he deemed it a safe gamble for such a major move. From experience, Jimmy knew that the posh theatre was drawing just the crowd he intended to serve.

Following John Kelly's example, Jimmy selected an elegant former residence, a two-story home originally built by a wealthy jeweler, for his new establishment. The setting ensured a comfortable, cozy atmosphere with just the right tone. Jimmy also adhered to his father's tradition of retaining a loyal staff, offering attentive service and serving great steaks, along with the requisite generous pour of whiskey. While the popular silver-dollar-sized corn cakes and the Faucon salad remained, he expanded his menu to include lobster, lamb, shrimp cocktail, and other classic dishes.

As in all such semilegal clubs, the liquor bottles on display were labeled with real names, but anyone could purchase the liquor. Jimmy's friends in law enforcement had no trouble looking the other way, as they were fairly frequent imbibers themselves. Jimmy had learned his lessons well, and as a result, the people of Belle Meade made "Jimmy Kelly's place" their neighborhood favorite.

The main floor offered a spacious dining room, but only strangers and out-of-towners dined there. People "in the know" parked their cars in the back and entered through the rear entrance and went down to the basement. Under its low ceiling with its cedar support posts and tables topped with red-checkered tablecloths, they were sure to find their Belle Meade neighbors. The crowded basement had an exciting, slightly outlaw atmosphere. Being seen there brought cachet, even if it occasionally meant standing on Coca-Cola crates to avoid the rain-dampened floor.

Thankfully, such rain events were rare, but the list of celebrities who streamed into Jimmy's basement over the years was extraordinary. Jimmy welcomed such top stars as Dorothy Lamour, Al Hirt, Pete Fountain, Dinah Shore, Gene Autry, George Montgomery, Burl Ives, and and baseball player Billy Martin, not to mention Hank Greenberg and the entire Detroit Tigers team. "Jimmy's place" was fast becoming Nashville's premier restaurant.

When the Vanderbilt Commodores won the Gator Bowl in 1955, Jimmy treated the whole team to a celebratory dinner, and Vandy fans packed the place, reveling in the victory until the first rays of dawn.[23]

Chapter 38

THE PROBLEM WITH CRÊME DE MENTHE

Because so many prominent Nashvillians dined at Jimmy Kelly's, local law enforcement was generally permissive about its liquor service. But they had to make occasional shows of force. Jimmy counted the small fines as a normal business cost.

In 1957, however, a self-appointed vigilante constable named Floyd Peck set his sights on Jimmy Kelly's. No one recognized him when he came into the restaurant, because he was far from his legal jurisdiction. He ordered a rum and Coke, and as soon as his drink was served, he stood and shouted, "This is a raid!" Then he promptly arrested the waiter and Jimmy Kelly.

This was not the first of Peck's lone-wolf operations, nor the first time he'd arrested people without jurisdiction. His exploits drew laughter from his peers, and he'd recently been dismissed from his job for failing to post the necessary bond. As usual, the arrests he made that day were quickly overturned, and for the next week or so Jimmy had to endure a good deal of ribbing from his buddies.

In downtown Nashville, John Kelly's original speakeasy, the old 216 Club, was still flourishing under Bob Woolwine's management. This was about the time my father, Bill Kelly, joined the family business, working first at one restaurant, then the other, wherever he was needed most. I was just a little boy then, but I well remember sliding down the staircase banister at the 216 Club.

The downtown restaurant still enjoyed a robust lunch and afterwork crowd, and still hosted the "Friday Night Club." It remained open until the wee hours to serve late-night musicians. I was told all the stories about famous guests. Frank Sinatra came there with Dean Martin, and that's where "Ol' Blue Eyes" tasted his first sip of Jack Daniel's. Elvis Presley and Johnny Cash were another pair of regulars, and the list goes on.

But without warning in 1962, an overzealous county sheriff raided the 216 Club and arrested Bob. The sheriff insisted on demanding that the so-called private bottle owners whose names appeared on the bottles would have to come downtown and claim their property. Many friends had allowed Bob to use their names over the years, and they considered the charade to be a huge joke. Lay claim to free booze, what could be better? But the joke didn't go over so well when Bob had to call Jimmy and tell him what had transpired.

While Bob was still posting bond to get out of jail, Jimmy drove downtown to oversee the strange episode, and he was still grumbling when one of the last customers arrived to collect his bottle. This gentleman, a local bank president, had been a 216 regular for years. As soon as he saw the bottle that bore his name, his eyes widened in surprise. He turned to Jimmy with a good-natured grin and said, "Jimmy, I don't mind that you used my name, but did you have to put it on a bottle of crēme de menthe?"

Chapter 39

JIMMY HOFFA'S NASHVILLE TRIAL

During 1962 and 1963, the president of the International Brotherhood of Teamsters made numerous visits to Nashville, and quite often, he and his entourage had dinner and drinks at Jimmy Kelly's in Belle Meade. He would usually arrive in a sleek red Thunderbird chauffeured by the chief of the Teamsters' local office. Of course, Jimmy welcomed the labor leader as graciously as he did everyone else, but these particular visits were a dubious honor. The man's name was James Riddle Hoffa, and he was facing a trial for corruption in Nashville's federal court.

US attorney general Robert Kennedy had been after Jimmy Hoffa for years. While serving as chief counsel to the McClellan Senate Committee investigating labor corruption, Kennedy had taken Hoffa to trial twice previously. Both times, Hoffa had gotten off. This time, in Nashville, Kennedy was determined to make the charges stick.

Hoffa laughed at the idea, because his 1.7 million Teamsters members gave him what he thought was invincible power. He told the Nashville press, "Bobby Kennedy is using the FBI as his own personal police force. He's starting out just like Hitler did."[24]

In the Nashville court, Hoffa was accused of taking bribes from a Michigan trucking company in return for calling off a strike. Kennedy had evidence that one million dollars had been channeled to Hoffa through a dummy Nashville company called Test Fleet Corporation, allegedly owned by Hoffa's wife and the wife of a close associate.

Kennedy had friends in Nashville, notably attorneys John Hooker Sr. and his son, John Jay Hooker Jr. Kennedy also knew *Tennessean* editor John Seigenthaler, a member of the Kennedy inner circle and Bobby's former aide, who reportedly ghostwrote Kennedy's book, *The Enemy Within*, about the McClellan Committee's work. During the course of the investigation, Kennedy named the senior Hooker to serve as the government's chief special prosecutor.

On the defense side, Hoffa also needed a local attorney and asked all the top names in town, but no one would take the case until a rising young star named Z. T. Osborn ultimately said *yes*, against the advice of Mr. Hooker. Osborn should have listened, because in the course of defending Hoffa, he became implicated in jury tampering and wound up disbarred and imprisoned, though he claimed to the end that he'd been entrapped.

In another shocking development, a former mental patient entered the courtroom and shot Hoffa with a gas-powered pellet gun. The pellets bounced off the stocky Hoffa, who then proceeded to kick, punch, and brutalize his would-be assassin until the bailiffs restrained him.

Everyone in Nashville followed the sensational trial, which made headlines in the local newspapers every day. And each time Hoffa appeared at Jimmy Kelly's, heads turned and whispers stirred the air. Hoffa had grown more famous—or infamous—than a Hollywood movie star.

The Test Fleet case eventually ended in a deadlocked jury and mistrial, but the judge ordered further investigation. In mid-1963, Hoffa returned to Nashville to plead not guilty. Due to the extensive local coverage of the first trial, the case was moved to Chattanooga, a change of venue that came as a relief to Jimmy Kelly and his staff. Though his customers loved to gawk at the villainous union boss, Hoffa made the waiters uneasy.

The Chattanooga jury found Hoffa guilty, and he was sentenced to eight years in prison. He fought the charges all the way to the Supreme Court, and in 1971, President Nixon granted him a highly controversial pardon. Hoffa immediately tried to regain control of the Teamsters, but on July 30, 1975, he went to Detroit to meet some associates and was never seen again.

Chapter 40

FINALLY! LIQUOR-BY-THE-DRINK IN NASHVILLE

The decade of the 1960s brought another turning point in American history and to the Kelly family business as well. Rising Cold War tensions, the Cuban Missile Crisis, Israel's Six-Day War, and Mao Zedong's cultural revolution in China formed a stressful backdrop to the graphic TV coverage of the Vietnam War and deadly violence at home, including the assassinations of the Kennedys, Malcolm X, and Martin Luther King Jr. Social movements such as the anti-war protests, civil rights marches, and the nascent women's movement were shaking up virtually every aspect of society.

Yet the sixties were also a time of economic prosperity, and families watched with pride as Neil Armstrong planted an American flag on the moon. Under President Lyndon Johnson's "Great Society" campaign, cities were remaking themselves, bulldozing hundreds of thousands of aging houses to make way for new construction.

One victim of these changes was the 216 Club, whose building was tagged for demolition under urban renewal. With the club's passing in 1965, a little bit of wild old Nashville passed away too.

All the same, my uncle Jimmy and my father, Bill, were full of optimism. They and other civic leaders had a new vision for Nashville, and they were actively working to attract new businesses, talent, and investments. In 1962, Davidson County voted to establish the "Metro Charter," consolidating city and county governments into one, to make the community more robust and efficient.

Soon after, a group of astute businessmen recognized another key change had to be made before Nashville would truly become a modern city. They knew investors from New York, Chicago, Los Angeles, or London would not want to be entertained in a quasi-legal bottle club that police might raid at any moment. Nor would convention-goers or tourists want to take such a risk. To compete on the national stage, Nashville had to finally move past Prohibition and legalize liquor-by-the-drink.

This small group of businessmen formed a secret society to work behind the scenes guiding Nashville toward a more sophisticated future. Comprising about twenty of Nashville's most powerful CEOs, bank presidents, attorneys, and university chancellors, the group called themselves "Watauga," after the historic Watauga Association founded in 1772 in East Tennessee, considered by prominent historians to be the earliest democratic government formed by American colonists.

Nashville's Watauga members swore a pledge of anonymity and altruism, promising to leave their own self-interests at the door and to focus only on improving the city. They met monthly over breakfast or lunch, and since they kept few written records, their vast influence on Nashville's direction was not revealed until many years later.

Among their achievements were the creation of the Metro Airport Authority, Leadership Nashville, and the Davidson County Group, which fostered relations between Black and white leaders. However, Watauga's campaign to legalize liquor-by-the-drink pitted the group against many of city's powerful conservative churches. The nation's two largest Protestant denominations were both headquartered in Nashville, so legalizing liquor-by-the-drink was a hard, uphill fight.

Watauga worked closely with two key leaders in its pro-liquor campaign: founding Watauga member Nelson Andrews, a noted real estate developer and civic leader, and political operative Eddie Jones, who headed the Chamber of Commerce and served as Watauga's de facto chief of staff. Jones would eventually become editor of the *Nashville Banner*.

A third pro-liquor advocate was the formidable Democratic fundraiser H. E. Flippen, owner of the Clark Hardware Company, and sometimes called the "power behind the throne" of Mayor Beverly Briley. Known to everyone as Mr. Flippen, he once told a reporter, "It was a gradual thing . . . I don't know how it happened that I became somewhat of a clearinghouse among varied interests in the community."

That was an understatement. According to city records, Mr. Flippen, as a private individual, decided which architects, insurance companies, and contractors the city would employ, who would be promoted in the police and fire departments, and who would be appointed to city boards, commissions, and authorities. Mr. Flippen took a hand in city real estate deals and rezoning decisions and directed millions of dollars in city expenditures. Though he enriched himself in the process, many viewed him as a force for good, because the city flourished under his behind-the-scenes leadership.

Mr. Flippen, Nelson Andrews, and Eddie Jones were all regulars at Jimmy Kelly's, as was Mayor Briley, a man who kept liquor on ice in his city hall office. Since a majority of Watauga members lived in Belle Meade and dined at Jimmy's place every week, their discussions often took place in one of Jimmy's private dining rooms.

To promote liquor-by-the-drink, the Chamber of Commerce established a committee chaired by attorney Charles Cornelius, which was comprised almost entirely of Watauga members. They hired Eddie Jones as their lobbyist. His first task was to change state law so counties could decide the question by referendum. Jones enlisted the help of the powerful lieutenant governor Frank Gorrell, perhaps the only man who had backdoor access to Governor Buford Ellington.

Together, they cut a deal with a swing-vote legislator who opposed all forms of liquor. This teetotaler agreed to support the referendum law, only if he could attach an amendment allowing counties to return to complete prohibition if they so wished. It was a gamble, but Jones and Gorrell said *yes*, believing such an amendment would be declared unconstitutional. And so it was. The referendum law was enacted without the amendment, and the teetotaling legislator could do nothing but fume.[25]

As soon as the law passed, Nashville leaders scheduled their referendum for September 28, 1967. But rival city Memphis—the state's largest city at that time—wanted to be first, so they scheduled their referendum two months earlier, in July. When the Memphis measure failed by ten thousand votes, Watauga members grew seriously concerned.

Nelson Andrews had been diligently organizing wards to get out the vote, especially in the affluent, pro-liquor suburbs. But he and Jones decided this might not be enough. Several weeks before the referendum, they met with Mayor Briley and Mr. Flippen, and Eddie Jones came up with an inspired idea. He said they should "make it impossible" to buy a drink in Nashville for a while.

Mayor Briley laughed and nodded, and the four men set to work planning the details. After the meeting, Briley dispatched an order to his police chief. "For the last two weeks before voting day, no whiskey will be sold in Nashville."[26]

I'm told it was Mr. Flippen who brought the news to Jimmy Kelly. He entered the club that same afternoon and asked Jimmy and my father, Bill, to join him for a private talk. The Kellys had been supporting the referendum all along, so the first thing Jimmy did was to pull out his checkbook.

"How much more do you need?"

Mr. Flippen shook his head. "I haven't come for another donation. It's something else."

When he explained the plan, Jimmy practically levitated out of his chair. "Two weeks! Do you know how much money I'll lose? Please let me write a check instead."

While Mr. Flippen patiently explained why the plan would work, Jimmy kept running his fingers through his hair, calculating the losses, and shaking his head.

Beside him, Bill spoke quietly. "It's OK, Mr. Flippen. We'll take care of it."

Over the next several days, Mr. Flippen and the others made many such visits to Nashville bars. As a result, in the final two weeks leading up to the vote, the citywide ban held firm. Jimmy Kelly's and even the Belle Meade Country Club went dry. And for once, the rival *Tennessean* and *Nashville Banner* newspapers united to support a political issue—liquor-by-the-drink.

Nevertheless, conservative clergymen and others raised a large war chest to fight against the "wets," and both sides bought TV airtime on the night before the vote. Their half-hour advertisements were slated to run back-to-back, and a coin toss decided the order. The pro-liquor ad would run first. Watauga recruited a renowned Nashville publicist, Hal Kennedy, to write the script, and they convinced popular country star Eddy Arnold to give an endorsement. With heartfelt emotion, Arnold talked about his worries for his teenaged son and why Nashville needed legally regulated liquor-by-the-drink. Jones said the spot brought tears to his eyes.

Then, legend has it, Hal Kennedy undercut viewership for the opposing ad, which was to follow. He did this by filling the last three minutes of his pro-liquor spot with tedious agriculture footage of boll weevils munching cotton squares (buds). Jones later told a reporter, "You could almost hear TV sets clicking off all over town." It was brilliant.[27]

When election day arrived, so many thirsty people were irate about the liquor ban that the "wets" won by a comfortable margin. And for the first time since the Tennessee bone-dry law in 1917, the Kelly family business would be operating completely within the law.

That singular referendum in 1967 launched the beginning of Nashville's rise to national prominence. As soon as liquor-by-the-drink became legal, more first-rate hotels sprang up, and large organizations starting choosing the city for conventions. As the "Nashville Sound" achieved international appeal, tourists flocked to the Opry and the city's many other music venues. Major businesses established branches in Nashville as well as corporate headquarters. Vanderbilt University Medical School and Meharry Medical College became incubators for the city's robust health-care industry. Young people moved in, bringing fresh talent and ideas from the far corners of the nation, and Nashville surpassed Memphis in size.

Today, Nashville ranks near the top of almost every list as a friendly, livable city with healthy job growth and new business starts.

Yet even after that game-changing referendum, Jimmy Kelly's 216 Dinner Club on Harding Road retained a hint of the charming old bottle club. Despite the club's enduring success, Uncle Jimmy still found reason to grumble about expenses. It turned out the new law included a tax on liquor-by-the-drink, and Jimmy was often heard to say, "You should've seen the profits back before the damn liquor taxes!"

PROLOGUE TO AN EPILOGUE

By Bo Roberts

As I entered the new COVID-driven entrance to Jimmy Kelly's Steakhouse, I checked in at the desk and headed toward the bar area where I was to meet two iconic Nashville figures for dinner—Mike Kelly, the proprietor, and Tom Ingram, the political guru who made the restaurant his unofficial Nashville office—I was interrupted by some other icons.

Having cocktails on the evening before a meeting were the organizers of The Has Beens (a group of which I was a member): Jimmy Naifeh, the retired Tennessee House of Representatives member who had been the longest-serving speaker of the house in history (a Democrat); Bill Purcell, who served as majority leader for several years under Naifeh and later stepped down (according to Naifeh) to become mayor of metropolitan Nashville for eight years (a Democrat); and Jim Henry, who served for years as minority leader, then a commissioner and deputy to the governor/chief of staff to Governor Bill Haslam (both

Republicans). We chatted briefly before I made my way to the bar area.

Then, working my way to the back of the room where Ingram and Kelly were holding the fort, I chatted briefly with bar visitors who included a key commissioner in Governor Bill Lee's administration, two longtime political leaders, and others. Later, after connecting with Tom and Mike, we were seated a few feet from another bar table where a group of political and government leaders was gathered.

All of this on a rather nondescript Tuesday night in December.

Tom, Mike, and I finally settled in to discuss the reason for our meeting: to talk about the closing chapter of Mike Kelly's fascinating book about the history of Jimmy Kelly's Steakhouse. We were to explore ways that I might help to convey the "modern" Jimmy Kelly's through Tom Ingram's prejudiced eyes about how much of Nashville's and Tennessee's history and future were shaped and influenced by the space, people, and atmosphere of this—dare I use the term that will soon be redundant with this story—iconic restaurant.

While discussing some of the history, we were interrupted twice by two different ladies who apologized but wanted to thank Mike for providing them a go-to place after they and their husbands had moved to Nashville (one was from Los Angeles; the other didn't say). I had had that experience with Mike before, and I'm sure Tom couldn't count the number of times it had happened.

The result of our conversation, and an ultimate consideration, is that I would attempt to convey Mike's and Tom's thoughts, along with those of some other icons, about what this restaurant is all about.

Unfortunately, the property that housed Kelly's Steakhouse in Belle Meade was going to be sold. Aware that the family was going to have to relocate its "heirloom" business, the younger Kelly volunteered to assist his father in scouting out the perfect new place from which to reimagine, recast, and relaunch the next incarnation of Nashville's most venerable steakhouse.

It was 1982, and Mike Kelly, who had been dutifully working at the restaurant, chopping lettuce and wrapping potatoes in aluminum foil since he was nine years old, had ultimately decided to forge a different career path in life. The Father Ryan High School graduate pursued a degree in communication design and art history at the University of Tennessee in Knoxville, where he eventually earned his degree. There he met, and later married, a tall, willowy blonde named Cathy Quillman. Before their marriage, he was employed by one of the industry's trendsetting firms in environmental wayfinding systems, headquartered in Connecticut. The company's leader took the best and brightest of her senior designers to Maine in the summers, which is where the Kellys spent their honeymoon and discovered a mutual love for the forests and islands of Maine.

The Kellys were lured back to Nashville when Kelly accepted an offer to work with the young architectural firm Gresham Smith, which was designing for Hospital Corporation of America, the massively successful healthcare company that would become synonymous with Nashville. Interestingly, the GSA offices were kitty-corner across the street from what would eventually become the new location of Jimmy Kelly's. The hunt for the next place to hang the Jimmy Kelly's Steakhouse sign would conclude with the acquisition of the Ridley Wills (one of the founding families of Nashville's National Life and Accident Insurance Company) home on Louise Avenue.

Kelly assisted his dad making the selection, and then interfaced with talented, Memphis-based consultant Herbert L.V. Hughes to appropriately retrofit the building, which was constructed in 1911. Even though, in hindsight, Kelly says that they would do it differently now, the "old" Jimmy Kelly's closed on a Saturday night and reopened the following Monday, September 13, 1982, in its new space.

For the first six months following the reopening, Mike helped out after work, doing what he terms "running the floor" each night. Because he felt called, enticed, slightly trapped, lured, and completely beholden to the family legacy, Mike eventually reached the conclusion that the time had finally arrived—he went to work full time for his dad, and with his "extended family," aka, the employees, in 1982. Then in February 1984, his mom and dad took their annual vacation to Florida and, as their son humorously characterizes it, they "never came back."

The third generation of the Kelly family now officially had control of the reins,, and the full weight of responsibility was on their shoulders. Having started working at the restaurant when he was just nine years old, busing tables, chopping lettuce for salads, and wrapping potatoes in foil for baking, Mike was truly back where he had originally begun. Fittingly, it was now his turn to offer his congenial smile and generous pours to the folks who would be arriving at his "home" in search of dinner and drinks.

As related by several of those enduring guests, along with his colleagues, Jimmy Kelly's was, and still is, a thoroughly enjoyable, comfortable watering hole.

Spurred first by the Belle Meade/Harding Road regulars who loyally chose to bring their business two and a half miles toward town to the Vanderbilt area, business was brisk from the start. With its relocation, an unusual phenomenon expanded the restaurant's customer base—diners from Mt. Juliet, Hendersonville, and other outlying areas began feeling as though Jimmy Kelly's was "their place" too. Being in proximity to hotels that were either adjacent to or located right downtown also dramatically expanded the number of reservations coming in from out-of-town visitors.

Politicians and business leaders had long made Jimmy Kelly's one of their regular favorite hangouts, but its move several miles closer to Capitol Hill increased its accessibility for many.

There have been dozens upon dozens of fabled figures who've comprised the clientele at Jimmy Kelly's over the past eighty-eight years, some of whom have even shared their thoughts "on the record" here. But there are also numerous tales about the restaurant that seem either so improbable or so outlandish, it's clear they can't possibly be anything other than the pure, unvarnished truth. Herewith is just a taste of one of those tales involving a figure who is, regrettably, no longer with us. Hopefully, though, he is looking fondly down upon us.

RAY BELL

Before he passed away in 2010, Ray Bell was a literal and figurative force in the state of Tennessee. He single-handedly built Bell Construction into one of the region's most respected contractors, erected such iconic structures as the AT&T building (more commonly known as the "Batman building") in downtown Nashville, and was responsible for building major highways and bridges throughout the state. Though he never ran for public office, Bell was a gale-force wind of political influence, a dynamo to be reckoned with, and a person of considerable power. His support was sought by many for his financial contributions, his formidable energy, his sphere of influence, and his genuine and abiding interest in nonprofit causes. He was also known for his short fuse, which occasionally propelled him headlong into the danger zone—a place where grown men can be so pigheaded as to forget that fisticuffs are never appropriate.

An example of what Bell's supremely supportive friendship could mean, however, was amply demonstrated during then-Speaker of the House Ned Ray McWherter's first run for governor of Tennessee in 1986, following fourteen years as Speaker. Among Bell's significant contributions was providing McWherter with full-time use of his private plane during the campaign. Speaker McWherter also held numerous fundraising breakfasts at Jimmy Kelly's, a time of day that Bell alleged was selected because "Ned Ray was too tight to buy liquor to serve his contributors," according to Kelly.

Bell's penchant for confrontation caught up with him one night in the bar at Jimmy Kelly's. An excited, well-oiled crowd had gathered there in anticipation of a victory in Nashville's referendum vote on whether or not to bring the Tennessee Titans (then known as the Houston Oilers) to town. The bar was jammed with jubilant supporters, but, as the generous pours continued, Bell's mood, for reasons unknown, began to darken as he recalled a lingering, unresolved issue between himself and Dave Cooley, deputy to then-mayor of Nashville Phil Bredesen. Their discussion about the matter soon overheated, with Bell unwisely attempting to take a punch at the reserved but very tough Cooley. A former, highly accomplished Golden Gloves boxer, Cooley deftly dodged Bell's amateur swings, and with a couple of well-placed countermoves, brought the encounter quickly to a close. Word of that incident—one of a very few at Jimmy Kelly's that burst through the "Code of Silence"—spread faster than a spark of fire on a dry forest floor. Somewhat surprisingly, the better part of valor eventually prevailed, which allowed a certain cordiality between the two. Both gentlemen continued to patronize Jimmy Kelly's.

Bell, in fact, was noted for having "his table" at the restaurant in the bar area, where he held court with various and assorted friends and associates three or four nights a week. Kelly, when recalling Bell's constant presence, said his table's location didn't conflict with the other "permanent table holder," Tom Ingram, because Ingram wanted to be in the corner to see who was coming in, while Bell preferred the other corner where he could keep one eye trained on the television screen.

Bell's absence during hunting season made for a more subdued atmosphere in the bar at Kelly's. Occasionally, Kelly would feel obligated to join Bell out in the field during duck season. The two often paired up during "Football Time in Tennessee," taking Bell's plane to Knoxville on fall football Saturdays to cheer on the UT Volunteers from Bell Construction's skybox in Neyland Stadium.

There's a multitude of Ray Bell stories, but another classic moment occurred late one night by accident. Mike Kelly had checked the restaurant as usual before closing. He saw that Little Joe had already departed for the night, so he turned off the lights and went home to bed.

At 5:30 a.m. Kelly was awakened by a phone call. When he answered, he heard a gravelly, whispery voice that he soon realized was Bell's. It seemed that Bell was phoning to ask Kelly if he could have a key to the restaurant. Finally, a groggy Kelly replied, "Well, I guess so, Ray. But why are you calling me at 5:30 in the morning to ask me that?" Bell responded sheepishly (or at least what passed as sheepish for him), "Because I am locked inside the damn place, and I don't want to set off the alarm and deal with the dog!"[28]

Kelly's head finally cleared enough to comprehend exactly what it was that Bell was trying to convey. Apparently, Bell had fallen asleep in the booth at "his table" in the bar. Kelly dutifully got up, got dressed, and drove downtown to rescue his wayward friend and devoted customer. That was an act that far exceeded a "generous pour," but made for a story worth telling for years to come.

TOM INGRAM'S PAST, PRESENT, AND FUTURE INTERTWINED WITH JIMMY KELLY'S STEAKHOUSE

Tom Ingram's first visit to Jimmy Kelly's Steakhouse was in 1979, when he and his young fiancée, Cindy, were escorted into the "regulars only" back entrance at Belle Meade's wildly popular evening meeting place on Harding Road.[29]

The couple was guided there by influential Belle Meade residents Luke and Susan Simons, the owners of the backyard where the couple was married, and where they had originally met. The 1979 version of Jimmy Kelly's was operated by Mike Kelly's father, Bill, and his uncle, Jimmy. Little did Ingram know then just how much the iconic institution would later become a central part of both his life and career. Ingram's introduction to Nashville came when his father, a Church of Christ minister, relocated the family to Tennessee's capital city.

Ingram's natural aptitude for writing emerged as a high school student. He captured the attention of acclaimed journalist John Seigenthaler, aka, "Seig," which was how many referred to the *Tennessean*'s famed young editor, who at thirty-six, was well on his way to becoming a legend. The association between the two men would eventually have a profound influence on Nashville and the country for decades to come.

Their meeting initially resulted in Ingram working part time at the *Tennessean* while hustling through Lipscomb University in three lightning-fast years. It was by happenstance that Ingram made his fortuitous entrée into political reporting. During a Lipscomb chapel service, Tennessee governor Frank Clement, a mesmerizing old-school politician, offhandedly mentioned (with regard to a US Senate seat run), "If this wasn't such a nonpartisan crowd, I would announce for political office today." Ingram, meticulous notes about Clement's comments in hand, went straight to the *Tennessean* to file the story.

Several hours later in Memphis, the governor was surrounded by an intense horde of reporters clamoring for verification of Ingram's story. When the governor indicated that he'd been misquoted, Ingram produced an audiotape. Nashville's morning paper-of-record featured a front-page confirmation of Ingram's original report in its next edition. That would not be the last time that Ingram would have an instrumental role in page one news.

His journalism career would eventually morph into a substantial political career when, in 1974, he accepted a position in Republican Lamar Alexander's gubernatorial campaign. However, it was Democratic congressman Ray Blanton who sailed into Tennessee's executive residence that November with a resounding 55.4 percent of the vote. While Alexander headed back to his law practice, the defeat saw Ingram pivot back to reporting when he accepted a job with the *Nashville Banner*.

By 1978, as the paper's chief political writer, Ingram was composing in-depth, full-page profiles about US senatorial candidates Jim Sasser and incumbent Bill Brock when he was summarily dismissed by a *Banner* executive. His refusal to alter Brock's profile almost cost him his job. However, the *Banner*'s publisher rehired him a few hours later, integrity still intact.

Two years later Ingram was back to work as a political operative during Alexander's second run for Tennessee governor. Working with Nashville's Holder Kennedy Agency, Ingram crafted Alexander's now-legendary campaign approach: the candidate would "Walk Across Tennessee" wearing a red-and-black flannel shirt. This bold strategy handily walked Alexander right into the governor's office with 55.8 percent of the vote (just a bit more than Blanton garnered in his winning gubernatorial race four years earlier), while earning Ingram an unassailable place on the life list of political gurus.

Having initially been named as the governor-elect's press secretary, Ingram's most significant assignment was to make a recommendation for Alexander's chief of staff. Following the submission of several candidates' names, the wily Ted Welch, Alexander's finance director and top advisor, persuaded Alexander to appoint Ingram instead. Welch conceived of a more substantial position: deputy to the governor, with the responsibility of "nothing to do every day except whatever the governor needs done." Ingram spent four eventful years in that role before transitioning back into the private sector.

Many years later he would be back at the helm for Alexander in Washington, serving as chief of staff for the man who had been elected to the US Senate. He remained inside "the Beltway" for seven years.

Through his public affairs consulting firm, Ingram would be heavily involved in the elections of other notable Tennessee politicians, including the late Senator Fred Thompson, Governor Don Sundquist, Senator Bob Corker, and Governor Bill Haslam.

While Ingram's relationship with Jimmy Kelly's Steakhouse had always been steady, his "residency" there began in earnest in 1996. That's when he was awarded a "permanent" seat in the bar at the table belonging to the indomitable Middle Tennessee commercial contractor Ray Bell. Ingram would later claim the Bell table as his own "permanent" spot, facing the original front door in Kelly's restaurant.

Ingram and Kelly affirmed that the most intense "residency" of all time was during the final six weeks of candidate Corker's 2006 senate campaign, when Ingram and his staff were working virtually around the clock. Ingram would call Mike—sometimes as late as 10:30 p.m.—and ask if he could, please, bring everyone over for dinner.

"Whenever I called, Mike would simply say, 'Come on over,' and we were treated as royally as if they had been patiently waiting all evening for us to arrive," Ingram said.

WHAT MAKES JIMMY KELLY'S SO SPECIAL?

Many have wondered if Ingram has a financial interest or an official tie to Jimmy Kelly's because he is seen occupying his table there so frequently. The answer is definitively no. But when he is there, he could be considered an unofficial cohost because he is certainly a confrere of Mike Kelly's, or, as he described it, "Mike is like a bro by a different mo."

Asked why Jimmy Kelly's is so special to him, Ingram outlines several additional reasons: The environment. Consistent food and service. And, of course, "the vibe," which includes an ironclad, unbreakable "code of silence."

"Whether a politician, a celebrity, a renowned musician, or a next-door neighbor, each is always a valued patron, but no one is ever exposed to anyone. Mike and his staff go out of their way to make everyone feel welcome. At the same time, they ensure that no one intrudes on anyone's time there," Ingram notes. "It's such a home away from home for me."

The notoriously tight-lipped Ingram—the former reporter who has been more accustomed to *asking* the questions rather than responding to them—can recount dozens of intriguing incidents that have transpired at Jimmy Kelly's, but it's not in his DNA to be particularly revealing.

This high-level political operative does, however, touch briefly on some of the hurdles that were surmounted in the Houston Oilers Tennessee relocation deal. It was 1995 and Ingram was sitting in the corner booth in Kelly's bar when he spoke to his client, Jim Haslam, founder of the nation's largest chain of fueling locations, collegiate gridiron star, and staunch East Tennessee Republican. Information was emerging that there was widespread concern among those supporting a professional football team for Tennessee that the idea could be in danger of falling apart.

It seems that Nashville's Democratic mayor at the time, Phil Bredesen, and Don Sundquist, Tennessee's Republican governor, were not on especially good terms. In the fall of 1994, Sundquist had triumphed over Bredesen in a divisive gubernatorial contest with 54.3 percent of the vote. Their lack of cordiality looked as though it might negatively impact the Oilers move—a Bredesen initiative—because bringing the bill to fruition was going to take a $77 million state bond issue. Sundquist's support was crucial in order to coalesce the legislative backing needed. Together, Ingram and Haslam devised a crafty rescue plan.

Not surprisingly, it goes without saying that on almost any night of the week, there will be *something* happening at Jimmy Kelly's.

CATHY THOMAS

It was a lunch meeting at Jimmy Kelly's Steakhouse (which happened to be on her birthday) that veteran fundraiser Cathy Thomas will never forget. It was also a lunch that in many ways changed the course of history in Nashville and in Tennessee.

Businessman and political insider Johnny Hobbs was hosting a private luncheon for about a dozen Nashville leaders in an upstairs room at Kelly's. He had invited them to meet Thomas's friend and client Phil Bredesen. Coincidentally, she received an important call during the gathering from Bredesen's chief advisor and supporter, Dave Cooley, who had significant information to convey. It was a fateful Tuesday—June 12, 1990—when current Nashville mayor Bill Boner, who had been sustaining multiple political "injuries" as the city's chief executive, announced that he would not stand for reelection. Upon relaying the content of Cooley's call to the group, host Hobbs turned to Bredesen and announced with great bravado: "Welcome, Mayor Bredesen!"

As has often transpired at Jimmy Kelly's Steakhouse, a political career found new life and continued. Bredesen had not been victorious in either of his two previous political challenges: he was defeated by Boner in the race for mayor and by Congressman Bob Clement in the race for the 5th District seat. Boner's capitulation on that day would ultimately spur the reenvisioning and the total revitalization of downtown Nashville during Bredesen's two terms as mayor, and later secure the state's long-term financial stability during Bredesen's eight years as governor.

That such a monumental moment occurred at Kelly's was entirely fitting, as it had been the central gathering place for Thomas throughout her career as chief fundraiser for former senator Jim Sasser (whom she also served on his Tennessee staff), former governor Ned McWherter, former congressman John Tanner, former congressman Lincoln Davis, and former congressman and senator Al Gore, among many others. Thomas has always held events or meetings at Jimmy Kelly's, which she calls her "homeplace–Cheers bar." It retains that status today as it remains the frequent roost for her and husband, Bob.

"I love Jimmy Kelly's!" said the effervescent, never-met-a-stranger Thomas. "When I go there, the people make me feel like they love me. I've never left there feeling unhappy," she noted with a laugh.

She also hosted her momma's last restaurant experience there, just a few days before her mother passed away in 2021. Thomas recalled being there with her mother during the previous holiday as part of her family's seasonal ritual of dining at Jimmy Kelly's amid the fabulous decorations. The exceptional dĕcor is a standing tradition, personally designed and overseen by Mike Kelly, who lets his artistic flair shine. She noted that families would come in and inquire about taking photos in front of the magnificently decorated tree (without sitting down to eat), and that Kelly, the epitome of Southern gentility, would welcome them with as much cordiality as he did his paying customers.

Kelly added that Thomas has long delighted in introducing others, especially young people, to the Kelly's experience. He said many of those Thomas "legacies" often returned with their parents and routinely became regulars themselves over the years.

Thomas's enthusiastic assessment: "It's a special, comfortable, laughing-out-loud kind of place."

BOB BALLOW

Accepting the title of the "longest-standing customer" at Jimmy Kelly's Steakhouse is an honor that acclaimed Nashville attorney Bob Ballow is more than delighted to accept.

"My first meal at Jimmy Kelly's was in September of 1950, soon after I started my freshman year at Peabody College," said the Nashville native.

Ballow noted that he and his college buddies continued to gather there (in the basement, entering through the back door "regulars" entrance at the Harding Road location) at least twice a week.

After completing a two-year stint with the US Navy, Ballow worked his way through the Nashville School of Law, married Betty, and moved to the neighborhood of Hillwood in West Nashville. The new couple continued the relationship that Ballow had already established with the restaurant, which he describes as "the best steakhouse in America."

Ballow, who has been listed in *Best Lawyers in America* since 1982, and named to the *Nashville Post*'s "Top 101 Lawyers," says he has traveled to all fifty states in the US. He adds that he has dined at steakhouses everywhere, and stresses that his judgment has never wavered.

Even when Jimmy Kelly's relocated to Louise Avenue, Ballow points out that the couple's dining routine didn't change. "Our habits stayed the same, we just changed locations," he said.

When queried as to whether he had sampled everything on Kelly's menu, he paused momentarily before responding, and said yes, he had. He related that just two days earlier (in April of 2022) he had ordered the crab cakes. Enthusiastic individual that he is, and apparently has always been, he indicated that they were "the best doggone crab cakes" he'd ever eaten.

Ballow says he routinely took clients from around the world to Jimmy Kelly's, all of whom "loved the Nashville experience with its friendly, welcoming service." He said it wasn't unusual for clients who had employees or friends planning trips to Nashville to call and ask, "What's the name of that great restaurant you took us to?"

It goes without saying that the employees at King & Ballow, the storied Nashville law firm he founded with partner Frank King in 1969, instinctively knew they would be receiving dinner for two at Jimmy Kelly's when it was time to celebrate their birthdays. "They loved it!" Ballow declared.

As Jimmy Kelly's longest-tenured customer, Ballow seems imminently qualified to deliver an assessment of Mike Kelly's performance in operating the restaurant in comparison with his uncle and his father. His verdict: very high marks.

And so the beat goes on for the man who has been dining at Kelly's for seventy-two of its eighty-eight years in existence. Congratulations, counselor.

MARY ANN McCREADY

Future powerhouse music industry executive Mary Ann McCready first experienced Jimmy Kelly's Steakhouse when she was a student at Vanderbilt. She vividly remembers walking into Kelly's thinking that it was the coolest speakeasy she'd ever seen. Nearly everyone who's ever been there would concur that McCready is right on point.

From the moment one steps on the sidewalk in front of the restaurant, Jimmy Kelly's exudes a vibe that suggests several things—it's a place with a deep, rich history; it has seen incredibly interesting times; and, while best behavior is welcomed and appreciated, whatever transpires within its walls will be received with customary Southern graciousness, within reason.

McCready, cofounder of Nashville's Flood, Bumstead, McCready & McCarthy, a nationally known entertainment business management firm, has been to Kelly's hundreds of times with clients, friends, and associates ("I don't discriminate," she noted). Her preferred seat is always in the bar area with her back against the wall, so that she can "watch everything that's happening . . . and things are always happening at Jimmy Kelly's."

The dynamic McCready said she has done some deals at Kelly's, but emphasized that what she finds even more compelling is observing others' business and political discussions from afar, as well as imagining the potential deal talks that might be going on. "I don't need to know exactly *what* is going on. I just enjoy *seeing* it going on," she confided in a mischievous tone of voice.

McCready said that one of her considerations when determining where to eat is: "How are we going to feel when we walk in? We always know how we'll be welcomed and treated at Jimmy Kelly's."

This current chair of the Country Music Hall of Fame and Museum's Board of Officers and Trustees also mentioned that it's not unusual to see celebrities dining at Jimmy Kelly's, and that some may be her guests. She doesn't worry about hosting there because of the "aura of borders." It is simply understood that the bright and famous will be free to enjoy their meal without interruption. "It's part of the atmosphere that is so comforting," she explained.

One of the all-time great stories about Jimmy Kelly's actually involved McCready's dinner guests. While she was entertaining a group of out-of-town business associates, one of the women in the party went upstairs to the ladies' room. On her return trip back downstairs to their table, however, she slipped on the stairs, turned a complete flip, and somehow landed upright and unharmed on her feet. "Everyone was amazed. She was just fine, but that episode was certainly the highlight of our meetings the next day!"

According to McCready, the "performer" was not an acrobat, but an agile financial advisor whose identity remains confidential. Mike Kelly confirmed, though, that as far as he is aware, this was the only known completed "flip" to have ever been landed, without incident, on the restaurant's thickly carpeted staircase.

Again, it was just another eventful evening inside the elegantly comfortable steakhouse on Louise Avenue.

DAVE COOLEY

In two consecutive years, Jimmy Kelly's Steakhouse hosted a pair of disparate, yet unforgettable celebrations commemorating major accomplishments in Nashville's history.

Dave Cooley, a political kingmaking,legislation-passing, policy-influencing legend himself, had managed Mayor Phil Bredesen's initiatives to attract an NFL team to Nashville, and, just a year later, worked to ensure the passage of an historic library program that featured a 300,000-square-foot main building as its centerpiece.

"Jimmy Kelly's was the perfect place for a group of sports fanatics and library zealots to join forces and push those landmark projects through," Cooley said in recalling those transformational moments from two decades ago. He said the Kelly family "home" has always been a natural habitat for gathering groups of all stripes, be they Democrats and Republicans or jocks and nerds. Cooley describes the restaurant as the ultimate "warm blanket of emotional comfort."

A Rockwood-raised, Tennessee Tech–educated, hard-driving, cool-under-pressure pro, Cooley and his wife, Melanie, who relocated to Nashville in 1986, were introduced to Jimmy Kelly's by Sharon and Mike Pigott, one of his early partners.

Cooley echoed the thoughts of fellow Roane Countian Jim Henry in referring to Jimmy Kelly's as an ideal location for developing relationships. Over the years, as both deputy to the city's mayor and deputy to the state's governor (Phil Bredesen), Cooley cited Kelly's as a perfect place to take economic development prospects in order to "build relationships that quite often resulted in mutually beneficial decisions for both parties."

In his business, Cooley Public Strategies, he said the restaurant is a go-to place for clients. "They can 'feel' Nashville and Tennessee here, enjoy the hospitality and, of course, the corn cakes."

Cooley says governors of other states always seem to feel quite at home at Kelly's too. He mentioned three he has taken there, including Bill Richardson of New Mexico, Brad Henry of Oklahoma, and Ronnie Musgrove of Mississippi. Most all of Cooley's out-of-town clients request Jimmy Kelly's in advance of their travel to Nashville.

In his longtime association with Bredesen, Cooley said they, too, had countless celebrations and numerous fund-raisers at Jimmy Kelly's over the course of twenty years. He summed it up by likening the Kelly experience to eating in "Nashville's dining room."

BRUCE DOBIE

Though he had been there several times before, Bruce Dobie's first major occasion at Jimmy Kelly's Steakhouse represented a seminal moment in the life of the young *Nashville Banner* reporter.

Four years after he started his career at the *Banner* in 1983, Dobie was engaged to Nashville mayor Richard Fulton's press secretary, Laura Lee Hardy. One of the first tasks the future bride and groom needed to address was bringing their parents together for that potentially awkward first dinner. With her parents residing in Kentucky and his in Louisiana, it wasn't as though the foursome were ever going to casually, naturally cross paths. Laura Lee's parents would be coming from Frankfort; his from Lafayette. The question of where the six of them would dine in Nashville was a big one. The pair chose Jimmy Kelly's.

"We wanted a nice restaurant, one that not only had good food, but was comfortable, and not stuffy. The choice seemed obvious. It proved to be among the best decisions we made as a couple," Dobie recalled. "It was a place where one wouldn't be ostracized if a little wine was accidentally spilled on the carpet."

By the mid-1990s, Dobie and his partner, Albie del Favero, had transformed a formerly listless weekly shopper, the *Nashville Scene,* into the new *Nashville Scene,* one of the most wildly successful alternative weeklies in the nation. The downside of that achievement was that someone had to shepherd their raging accomplishment to the printers every Tuesday night. Dobie, the University of the South graduate with the master's degree from Columbia University Graduate School of Journalism, obviously got that job. By the time the newly robust publication was ready to print four (sometimes five) times a month, Dobie had written and edited thousands of word and was within slumping distance of the term "brain-dead." With clockwork regularity, Dobie said he would manage to find his way to the end of Kelly's bar almost every Tuesday night through the year 2004. Lee, Kelly's stalwart bartender, would have Dobie's preferred cocktail, a perfectly crafted gin martini (garnished with the special olives that Dobie provided), waiting on the bar by the time he'd snagged a seat. In addition, his standing cheeseburger order would already be cooking on the grill as the first sip of that icy, gratifying martini was making its way down the back of his throat.

As Dobie rejuvenated his brain and body with sustenance and libations, he would entertain himself by keenly observing the nightly scene that was always unfolding in Kelly's bar. "It was fascinating to watch the different mix of the city and state's business and political leadership engaging in congenial conversation," Dobie noted.

One of the political traditions Dobie said he enjoyed most as a *Banner* staff member was the two papers' election night custom of a jointly hosted *Banner–Tennessean* newsroom buffet. Candidates and election workers were invited to drop by to celebrate or commiserate, depending upon their personal interest in the voting results. Once this practice ceased at 1100 Broadway, though, the *Scene* resuscitated the idea, putting its own imprimatur on it. They relocated the event to an upstairs room at Kelly's, elevated the food and drink, and brought in a large-screen television for viewing the results. "It was a lot of fun for the news team, and for most of the newsmakers," he said.

Whether entertaining future in-laws or seeking recovery from mental fatigue during the past three decades, Dobie has consistently found refuge and replenishment at Jimmy Kelly's. He has continued his Kelly's ritual as he's wrestled his latest media venture, *Power Poll*, into thirty markets (including his hometown of Lafayette, of course) from Texas to Illinois to California to Florida to Georgia and back. His company's three- to five-minute polls search the minds of community influencers for responses to thoughtfully posed questions regarding critical opportunities and issues in the cities of *Power Poll*'s 29,000 participants.

And yet, the one question that remains unanswered for Dobie is *which* brand of anchovy stuffed olives does he like best with his Kelly's martini? He's working on that.

DIANNE NEAL

Nashville attorney Dianne Neal's first visit to Jimmy Kelly's was at its Harding Road location in 1978. There, she joined fellow members of her disco class (a group of young married couples who'd managed to snag reliable babysitters for an evening out. Several in the group—the Nashville natives—had heard about Kelly's white-coated waiters and the old days when clients' labeled whiskey bottles were kept behind the bar. That night brought back memories of similar "private" clubs in East Texas, where Neal had been raised. The whiskeys were labeled there, too, and kept well out of sight, in anticipation of being served with the widely available prime Lone Star state beef.

This former member of the Tennessee State Ethics Commission and former chief counsel to Tennessee governor Ned McWherter met the distinguished, illustrious lawyer Jim Neal in a law firm library a decade later. Then, at a birthday celebration held in one of Kelly's private rooms a few weeks later, Neal asked if she would consider meeting for lunch. As his divorce was not "quite" final at the time, he noted that she could invite a friend to come along. She felt that his offer was "sweetly proper," and was delighted that, instead of focusing on the other glamorous women at the party, he had asked her—a then-fledgling legal counselor with "no resume," as she describes it—on a date. Despite Jim's distinguished, acclaimed career as prosecutor of labor leader Jimmy Hoffa and prosecutor of the Watergate break-in crimes, as well as the defense of Ford Motor Co. in the Pinto automobile criminal trial and the defense of Dr. George Nichopolous in the death of entertainer Elvis Presley, Dianne was determined not to be intimidated. And so she accepted his invitation. The couple was married for years before Jim passed away from complications of cancer in 2010.

She says that over the years, guests from Manhattan, Chicago, and Los Angeles would telephone on their first nights in town, asking to meet for dinner at—where else? Jimmy Kelly's, of course. Currently an instructor of law at the Nashville School of Law, Neal says she and Jim celebrated absolutely everything at Kelly's: winning (and sometimes losing) football games, birthdays, engagements, graduations, retirements, divorces, and grandchildren. Two of Jim's Vanderbilt Law School reunions, where members of the acclaimed class of 1957 convened, were also held upstairs at Kelly's.

When Jill Vollner Winebanks, Jim's assistant at the Watergate trial, visited Nashville recently, she invited Neal to dinner. When asked if she (Neal) should make reservations somewhere, Winebanks replied that she had "taken care of it, doing what Jim would have done . . . and booked a table at Kelly's."

JIMMY NAIFEH

While discussing his longtime relationship with Jimmy Kelly's Steakhouse, former Speaker of the Tennessee House of Representatives Jimmy Naifeh's eyes lit up. He was delighted to be sharing one of his favorite memories about Kelly's, which actually took place nearly two hundred miles west of Nashville. For more than twenty years, Speaker Naifeh led an annual fundraising event for St. Jude Children's Research Hospital, the internationally known facility in Memphis that treats children with cancer, free of charge.

Naifeh partnered with his fellow legislators to host the "Rural West Tennessee Shootout," a golf tournament held every year at Pickwick Landing State Park. The "West Tennessee Mafia" (as some of us folks from other parts of the state refer to them) held a fun, raucous event that generally netting approximately $80,000 for the hospital. The Speaker particularly wanted the Jimmy Kelly's connection highlighted—because Mike Kelly journeyed there, food and grill in tow, each and every year, to serve as the event's head chef, providing his time, equipment, and food at no cost to support the cause.

"Mike became such a fixture at this event that our guests would always ask if he was going to be there with the burgers and fixings," Naifeh fondly remembers.

Native West Tennessean Naifeh was born in Covington, raised there, still resides there, and represented the area in the state legislature for almost four decades. He served as Speaker of the House for eighteen years, holding that prestigious and powerful position longer than any other individual in Tennessee's history. He began his thirty-eight-year legislative career in 1974 and retired from the office, but not from politics, in 2012.

Naifeh still travels to Nashville quite frequently, where he has a gaggle of grandchildren and a legion of friends and associates. His visits to Davidson County customarily include a stop at Jimmy Kelly's.

He enjoys recalling the "good old days" when legislative committees were permitted to meet off-site. The bipartisan groups often had dinner in one of the restaurant's private rooms upstairs. Breaking bread together instinctively engendered relationships, creating friendships that endure to this day, according to Naifeh. "We all felt so welcomed by Mike and the great staff; it's such a comfortable, enjoyable place to be."

Naifeh smiles when looking back at the numerous after-event stops that occurred at Jimmy Kelly's. In particular were the post-Steeplechase gatherings. "I think it was a requirement when we were Ray's [Bell] designated guests at the annual Iroquois race in Nashville—we were to convene at Jimmy Kelly's following the meet. That was included in the marching orders." As Speaker, Naifeh was always highly respectful of standard procedure, so when commanded to appear at a certain place at a certain time, he dutifully complied. In this case, he did so happily, because there were few things that felt more natural than saying, "Hey, meet me at Jimmy Kelly's."

JIM HENRY

"I always feel comfortable at Jimmy Kelly's. It brings back the memories of 'practicing politics' there, when members of both parties felt at ease there *and* with each other," noted Jim Henry, an understated but quietly formidable force in Tennessee politics for decades.

Henry's foray into political leadership began when he was just twenty-six. He was elected to the city council in the small East Tennessee town of Kingston, where he became mayor at the age of twenty-eight. After serving nearly a decade in local government, this resident of predominantly Republican Roane County decided to run for the Tennessee House seat representing the 32nd District.

A University of Tennessee graduate, Henry came by his inclination to serve naturally. Following four years in the US Navy during Vietnam, he did post-military volunteer work with veterans and was inspired to follow the same path as two of his forebears: Peter Turney of Winchester, who served as governor of the Volunteer State from 1893 to 1897, and John F. Henry, a former Speaker of the Senate from Knoxville. Henry, who began serving parts of Roane, Morgan, Anderson, and Campbell counties as state representative in 1978, was elected as the House's Republican minority leader within twenty-four months of his arrival on Capitol Hill.

Tom Ingram, deputy to Governor Lamar Alexander (who had just been reelected to a second term), introduced the new minority leader to his favorite haunt in 1982, Jimmy Kelly's inaugural year. Like so many others who became regulars there, Henry immediately warmed to the gracious welcome from proprietor Mike Kelly and his staff.

"It was a gathering place for business and political leaders. It was, and still is, a place where you built relationships. Not a lot of policies or positions were discussed, but after you had a drink or dined with someone, you could still disagree with them. It was hard to attack that same person in another setting," Henry added.

When asked to comment on Ingram's label of "Code of Silence," Henry paused and said, "I would agree, but I would call it a 'Code of Congeniality' too." He observed that over the many years he had been a patron at Jimmy Kelly's, no matter how crowded the bar, no matter how many drinks had been consumed, he'd never witnessed anyone "get out of line or cause a disturbance."

After twelve years in the legislature, Henry returned to his hometown roots and went back to work in the private sector. And, though he had been relishing life on his rural farm, Henry agreed to "return to duty" when he was called back into public service by newly elected Republican governor Bill Haslam (2011–19). A young governor without statewide legislative know-how or the administrative experience of managing sprawling departments across ninety-five counties, Haslam wisely drew on the longevity and maturity of those who had served before him. Henry agreed to become the new governor's first commissioner of the Department of Intellectual and Developmental Disabilities. He would also serve as commissioner of the Children's Services department, before being elevated to deputy/chief of staff to the governor during Haslam's second term. His call to duty restored his regular visits to Jimmy Kelly's, especially on Tuesday nights during legislative sessions.

Henry recalled one very special evening at the restaurant when he and friends hosted John Jay Hooker, twice the Democratic nominee for governor of Tennessee, jurist, agitator, and bon vivant, in a delightful evening of storytelling, not long before Hooker passed away. He had gotten to know Hooker while both had been lobbying for the passage of "right to die" legislation (Henry was advocating as an individual, not as a member of the Haslam administration). It was a very personal issue for both men, and though unsuccessful—one of the few times his advocacy did not prevail—Henry hopes it might be revived someday.

Having Mike Kelly's restaurant as the backdrop for either a "last" or "first" experience is a frequent theme among those who have shared their recollections about this classic Nashville institution. And so it continues for Henry, his wife, Jeanne, and others today.

BUTCH ELEY

Although he was deep in the midst of shepherding a multi-billion-dollar state budget on behalf of Governor Bill Lee through Tennessee's General Assembly session, Butch Eley was definitely not going to miss out on talking about Jimmy Kelly's Steakhouse. He is a man who has the unenviable job of wearing two key, all-consuming business hats: one as Tennessee's commissioner of Finance and Administration and another as the state's deputy to the governor. Despite the phenomenal workload, Eley made a distinct point of carving out time to discuss Kelly's, which has special significance for him both in his business and political lives.

Eley especially wanted to talk about Kelly's "secret sauce." He said, "We aren't talking about a steak sauce; it's the quintessential host Mike Kelly, his staff, and the way they make everyone feel welcome, comfortable, and at home."

"It's a place to see and be seen, and where deals are sealed. People often say one could get a quorum there on any night of the week," Eley quipped.

The Cheatham County native made the short trek to Music City to earn his undergraduate and master's in business administration degrees from Belmont University. Following graduation, he experienced his first taste of government while working on Congressman Bill Boner's staff from 1982 until 1986. When Boner was elected mayor of Metro Nashville, Eley served as chief of staff during the first two years of his term. He then moved into the world of business, joining Tom Ingram at the Ingram Group.

That move alone exponentially increased his visits to Kelly's. And as if that weren't enough, the perpetually exacting Ray Bell became one of his clients, which meant he was fully and completely "Kelly-fied" and would be spending lots of time there.

Eley later donned his entrepreneurial hat and launched an innovative business called Infrastructure Corporation of America (ICA), which offered an array of services such as highway maintenance and operations to states and cities. Eley's all-star lineup of prominent Nashville investors included Bell, Tom Beasley, and Tom Cone. That trio of titans, who provided an abundance of support, guidance, and encouragement, met regularly with Eley at—you guessed it—Jimmy Kelly's. During the twenty-year period he owned ICA, prior to selling it a few years ago, Eley said he enjoyed a plethora of discussions and celebrations at Kelly's with the threesome, not to mention too many corn cakes to count. He still considers it to be his go-to place to relax and says one is as likely to "seal a deal" there as anywhere.

BILL AND MARY HANCE

More than fifty years ago, the "newbie" police reporter with the *Nashville Banner* heard about this place to get a good steak—and potentially pick up a good story, as well. Reporter instincts led Bill Hance in the back entrance to Jimmy Kelly's Steakhouse on Harding Road. When he entered he found a cacophonous bar in full evening swing and felt fortunate to find one empty seat available. He took in the atmosphere of Kelly's basement level, including its exposed overhead water pipes, and felt completely at home. The bartender asked what he'd like and then followed with, "I haven't seen you in here before. Are you a friend of Judge [so and so]? He would like you to have a drink from his bottle."

Hance didn't indicate whether he came across any leads that night, but he did find a place with a good steak, a generous pour, and plenty of potential news sources to tap in the future.

Mary Morton started her longtime relationship with Jimmy Kelly's as a young *Banner* reporter too. "As a starving reporter, it was a big night out for me; I always ordered the tiny filet, then filled up on the corn cakes." This pair of young reporters, who were married in 1982, has maintained its support of Jimmy Kelly's throughout the past four decades. After seventeen years at the *Banner*, Bill moved to Vanderbilt, where he served for twenty-five years as assistant vice chancellor of the Medical Center's office of news and communications. He now works up an appetite operating Billy's Corner service station in Sylvan Park.

When Mary migrated to the *Tennessean* in 1998, she took her already popular "Ms. Cheap" column with her, developing it into the paper's most read "advice" column ever. She describes Mike Kelly as "such a class act" in the myriad ways he quietly but very actively supports the community, including her annual "Penny Drive for Second Harvest."

"I love that Jimmy Kelly's represents 'old' Nashville, but is also poised for the future. And I still love the filets and corn cakes," she declared.

The couple also related that, "It's always fun to enjoy a glass of wine at the fabulous bar, where there is no telling what movers and shakers and politicians you might see."

Mary Hance said her Ms. Cheap Facebook page still alerts followers to the date that Jimmy Kelly's offers its half-off gift card.

"Long live Jimmy Kelly's!" she exclaimed.

HAL HARDIN

"It combines old-fashioned elegance with a *Cheers* bar atmosphere," according to eighth-generation Middle Tennessean Hal Hardin, who was first introduced to Jimmy Kelly's at its Harding Road location by his mentor, John Hooker Sr. Like many others, Hardin, too, entered through the "regulars entrance" in the back.

Hardin, who received his law degree from Vanderbilt, went on to be the presiding judge for the Nashville criminal courts and to become a noted federal prosecutor in the US Attorney's office, including during the infamous "coup" of the early swearing-in of Lamar Alexander to replace the increasingly unethical Governor Ray Blanton. He recalled several other iconic Nashville restaurants such as the Captain's Table, Highway 100 Supper Club, Julian's, and Arthur's, all of which have gone by the wayside while Jimmy Kelly's Steakhouse is celebrating its eighty-eighth year of continuing operation.

"To me, in addition to the good food, of course, I have always appreciated the waiters and employees there as they seemed to represent the very fabric of Nashville," Hardin, senior partner at Hardin Law, observed.

When queried about Tom Ingram's "Code of Silence" observation, Hardin said he had never thought of it in those terms, but said it does reflect an unwritten, family-type rule that brings an added comfort level to dining at Jimmy Kelly's.

Hardin also mentioned that one thing he still yearns for that was popular at Kelly's Harding Road location is Hooker Sr.'s favorite appetizer, the curiously named "Rat Trap Cheese and Pineapple." He said he occasionally raises the subject with Kelly. "I keep talking to him about it. Though it might not look too good on a menu, I'm going to bring some in and get him to try it, so that a few of us can secretly order it from the kitchen," Hardin said with a mischievous tone.

Like so many others, that's the kind of thing that only a family member could bring up.

BOBBY JOSLIN

"Daddy, don't you ever put me in that situation again!" shouted his daughter Kayla. "That was *the* mayor of Nashville."

The reprimand was delivered after a lengthy but exceedingly enjoyable evening at Jimmy Kelly's Steakhouse. The diners included Bobby Joslin; his wife, Vicki; daughter, Kayla; and Mayor Karl Dean, who joined the family on a Saturday night dinner while his wife, Anne Davis, was traveling out of town.

As the laughter-filled night wore on, the mayor released his security detail from duty, indicating that the Joslins had volunteered to take him home. Later that evening, with everyone in excellent spirits and in good shape (unless someone was keeping tabs on the specific number of sips taken from Kelly's delicious offerings that night), the adults were ready to be delivered to their respective domiciles. The only one not partaking of spirits was Joslin's sixteen-year-old daughter, who had a new driver's license and was anointed as the group's designated driver.

After safely transporting the mayor to his West Nashville home, Kayla gave her father a serious scolding. Not surprisingly, driving the mayor had made her a bit nervous. This was not the first time an event involving a mayor (or a mayoral candidate) at Jimmy Kelly's evoked strong emotions, but it may have been the first direct admonishment issued.

Joslin recalled that evening with a chuckle, as just one of the many humorous episodes that have occurred at his favorite "political hangout."

Before he became a regular, or a Kelly's "family member," as he describes it, Joslin got to know and became friends with Mike Kelly when he was working as a designer at Gresham Smith architectural firm, collaborating on a project for HCA. Then one day he learned Kelly had departed to take over his family's business, and their relationship transcended to the new location as well.

A disparate group of what Joslin calls "political hacks" gathers at Kelly's regularly, and he said "by the time we're on a second drink, we've already decided who the next mayor will be. Then we may gather again in a few days, and go in an entirely new direction." As a certified pilot, flight instructor, and former chairman of the Metro Nashville Airport Authority, Joslin knows a little something about heading in the right direction. The main point he wanted to emphasize was that, "No matter what party we represent or what faction, the thing that bonds all of us together is that we honestly care about what happens to our city."

The owner of the the immensely successful Joslin and Son Signs spoke for a lot of people when said that "the love of Nashville" supersedes any and all alliances.

"When you walk in the door, that greeting from Mike Kelly, in his suit and tie with his smiling face, sets the tone. It's cemented later on when he comes by your table to see if everything is okay. You feel comfortable, safe, and confidential while you're there. It's a true Southern meeting place with politics written all over it," he noted.

KARL DEAN

Reflecting on Jimmy Kelly's as a "special, special place," former Nashville mayor Karl Dean chuckled as he observed: "You know, I can't think of a time I visited Jimmy Kelly's where I was ever angry with anyone."

"First of all, when Anne [Davis, Dean's wife] and I go there, we always run into several people we know. Some of them never voted for me nor would ever, and while we might disagree on many things, in that atmosphere we could discuss things but never be disagreeable," Dean reflected.

When Dean won in the first round of voting to move forward into the runoff, he held his celebratory dinner upstairs at Kelly's, in the private rooms where friends, supporters, and staff could relax and share the joy of momentary victory. Seven weeks later, when Dean triumphed in the September 2007 runoff, Jimmy Kelly's was once again the go-to place for relishing the positive results.

Dean's original visit to the restaurant was with Anne and his future mother-in-law at the Belle Meade location (where they entered through the "regulars" back door, of course).

Kelly's became a regular favorite in its new location in 1982. Dean had been acquainted with Mike Kelly a bit over the years but related how he and Mike got to know each other much better once he initiated his race for mayor.

"Mike shared with me his reasons for supporting the proposed new convention center—campaign issue—and why it would be good for Nashville (and obviously his business). But he was also passionate about what that type of progress would mean to his bartenders, waiters, and other employees, as well as to the spirit of Nashville," Dean recalled. (Note: As mayor, Dean was extremely committed to what became the largest public investment of funds in Tennessee's history. The $600 million investment has been, and is, a tremendous success. Until the pandemic occurred, it had surpluses each year. It was able to ride out that major interruption primarily because of its earlier success.)

Why is Jimmy Kelly's Steakhouse so "special"? Dean recited: "The food, of course, the corn cakes, the uniqueness of the atmosphere, and the people... the people who work there, the people who eat there, and the individuals who almost seem to reside there."

BUTCH SPYRIDON

Admitting to having been "slightly overserved," Nashville tourism guru and leader Butch Spyridon climbed on top of the bar in (where else?) Jimmy Kelly's Steakhouse, raised his glass to the gathering of Nashville's vanguard, and shouted: "Nashville 3, Naysayers 0!"

Slightly chagrined as he recalls that precise moment in 2010, but joyful in remembering the occasion, Spyridon was toasting Mayor Karl Dean and the Metro Council members for giving their approval to the largest public project ever funded in Davidson County: the $600-million-dollar Music City Center (MCC). The celebration represented the third leg of an economic triad that has fed Nashville and Tennessee's tax coffers for the last quarter of a century: MCC, the NFL stadium, and the original multiplier, Bridgestone Arena.

Spyridon, CEO of the Nashville Convention & Visitors Corporation, spoke enthusiastically about the appropriateness of Jimmy Kelly's, with its status as one of Nashville's oldest and most most-enduring institutions, as being the ideal setting for rejoicing in the far-reaching decisions that were giving life to the "new, new Nashville."

When Spyridon arrived in Nashville in 1991, bringing an array of fresh ideas and approaches to creating and developing the city's brand and increasing visitor traffic, he already understood that he needed to seek out, learn about, and value the strands and fibers of history from which the traditions of "old Nashville" had been woven. Spyridon had moved to Music City from Baton Rouge, Louisiana, a place the French dubbed "Red Stick" in 1699 because of a boundary marker on the river bluff, so he was already well-versed in honoring and highlighting a city's historical antecedents. Baton Rouge was also the city where he learned a highly valuable lesson in relationship-building. He was at Phil's Oyster Bar & Seafood, a Baton Rouge landmark, when the owner invited him into the "backroom," which was regularly occupied by the state's governor, the city's mayor, the president of Louisiana State University, and even the LSU Bengal Tigers' football coach. As the proprietor escorted Spyridon into that room filled with boisterous patrons, the volume level noticeably dropped when he entered as all eyes turned to look him over. After a moment of nearly complete quietness, the owner yelled out: "This guy is OK!" The loud buzz in the room quickly returned, and Spyridon knew he had found his place.

The equivalent backroom place in Nashville was Jimmy Kelly's Steakhouse, and the equivalent owner was Mike Kelly. From Spyridon's point of view it was at that location, and through Mike's friendship and support, that much of Nashville's future was decided or, at the very least, influenced.

"It's institutional knowledge. It's an iconic representation of who and what Nashville is and what it could aspire to be," Spyridon said while explaining the special significance of a place like Jimmy Kelly's. He added that there were few people who were aware of the depth of the contributions that Mike Kelly and his institution have made and continue to make on behalf of the city he loves. Spyridon added that the extraordinary support he's received from people like Kelly, and fellow restaurateur Randy Rayburn, has enabled him to stretch for the kind of tourism and convention goals and benchmarks that, in earlier times, might have seemed unattainable. He also said that their open-minded approach and positive attitudes made his job both possible and much more enjoyable.

"How many decisions, deals, or ideas were fostered at 'the end of the bar' at Jimmy Kelly's?" Spyridon wondered aloud. Well, we know of at least one decision that gave him the moxie to climb atop that famous bar and proclaim victory.

PART OF THE JIMMY KELLY'S "FAMILY": ROBERT, ARTHUR, AND LEE

As much as the history of Jimmy Kelly's is about the founding Irish-American Kelly family itself, its broader "family" stories encompass the narratives of the diverse, dedicated individuals whose contributions have so clearly helped build the enduring spirit of this exceptional place.

Three current members of the Kelly's "family," all of whom provide the high standard of hospitality that compels diners to return dinner after dinner after dinner, weighed in on their loyalty to Kelly's. This particular trio has been cited by various guests as representing the essence of Jimmy Kelly's, and are seen as modern examples of why Jimmy Kelly's can boast of eighty-eight years in business.

One staff member has been featured in a full-page photograph in a book about the South, one has displayed his humor and engaging personality on radio and in television ads for "his home away from home," and one is featured in a country song, a fairly rare honor, even in a town nicknamed "Music City." Let's take an inside-looking-out peek.

ROBERT OLDEN

The senior member of this group, Robert Olden, with thirty-nine years of experience at Kelly's, plunked down a seven-pound, 384-page coffee-table book titled *Southbound: Photographs of and about the New South* (by Mark Sloan and Mark

Long) and turned to page 247. And there, in full color, was the elegant, white-jacketed Olden at a table in one of the historic upstairs rooms at Jimmy Kelly's. The 2018 catalogue of photographs, which accompanied an outstanding national touring exhibition, organized by the Halsey Institute of Contemporary Art at the College of Charleston, was obviously a prized possession of this veteran waiter and of the restaurant as well.

"I learned a long time ago that if you take care of people, they will take care of you. We do that here with good food at a reasonable price, looking out for what people want, not trying to sell them something," said the oft-requested scion of service.

Like so many of his guests, Olden says he is devoted to working at Jimmy Kelly's because "it's family," and feels like his "second home." He smiles when asked about some of his favorite guests—"there have been so many over the years." One who sprang immediately to mind was charming native Nashvillian and actress Reese Witherspoon, along with her family. Olden said he was glad to see her back and spending so much time in Middle Tennessee. Other favorites have included Tennessee speaker-then-governor Ned McWherter, Governor Bill Haslam, mayor-then-governor Phil Bredesen, and "on and on: just good people doing good things."

"It's part of me," Olden concludes about his relationship with Jimmy Kelly's.

And for nearly four decades, he has been a significant part of what Jimmy Kelly's is all about.

ARTHUR WHITE

When looking in the dictionary for the antithesis of "stuffy," one might well be lucky enough to find an image of Arthur White.

The vibrant, always smiling, three-decade veteran of Jimmy Kelly's waitstaff is a master of carefully and delicately deflating any reserved, stuffy, or self-conscious bubbles that might be hindering guests from having a completely rollicking good time should they so desire. (His regulars have long since abandoned all pretenses.)

It seems that owner Mike Kelly adjusted to this ball-of-fire waiter fairly quickly, because not too long after White joined "the family," he was quickly included in making radio and television commercials touting Jimmy Kelly's.

"No matter who Mike asks me to wait on, he always says, 'Arthur, just be Arthur, and do your thing.' I guess it's worked out OK," White recalls.

Before joining the Kelly's "family," White worked for several years at Opryland Hotel restaurants and enjoyed it but said he truly wanted to be part of a place that was a bit smaller and a little more personal. Jimmy Kelly's was the answer.

Several of Kelly's regulars, such as Bob Ballow and Cathy Thomas, specifically ask for White if they are going to be dining there on either of his regular Thursday or Friday nights. One of White's unique and unexpected experiences transpired a few years ago when then-US Speaker of the House John Boehner was frequently in Nashville. The two had a "lot of knee-slapping fun" that didn't reflect the somewhat reserved persona for which the GOP leader was generally known at the time.

"Nobody really wants to be uptight, so I try to let them be themselves by being who I am," he said just as owner Kelly was passing by. Kelly paused briefly to nod in total agreement.

"It's fun to watch our out-of-town guests become like home folks once they soak in Jimmy Kelly's atmosphere. They quickly see that they can have fun while enjoying a great meal," White said. "It's pretty special." His guests confide that they would put him in that category as well.

LEE PARRISH

The youngster in this trio is Lee Parrish, a twenty-two-year veteran of Kelly's and Tennessee native who was raised in Murfreesboro (but, coincidentally, born in the very same Nashville hospital as owner Mike Kelly). While attending Middle Tennessee State University, Parrish began working in the food and beverage industry to support his studies and reduce his student loan obligation. After a while, though, he realized how much he actually enjoyed it and decided to make it his career.

That pivotal decision would lead to him meeting all kinds of fascinating people, not to mention having his bartending skills become part of a country music song. The terrific tune was penned by longtime Jimmy Kelly's customer, successful songwriter Michael P. Heeney. He and his wife are regulars whom Parrish has gotten to know over the years.

Heeney wrote and produced a song entitled, "I Came Here to Drink." The opening verse:

"Lee, you make a good pour,
So pour me some more,
I Came Here to Drink"

There's no doubt, obviously, about who *the* Lee is, as he is now immortalized in the bartender's song parade.

Parrish came to Jimmy Kelly's after being burned-out on the business for a few months. He was biding his time working for a company that delivered lost luggage for airlines at Nashville International Airport. While waiting for luggage in the very early days of the year 2000, he ran into a friend who asked what he was doing. His friend told him to check with her friend, the head bartender at Jimmy Kelly's. In a fit of pique, an employee there had walked off the job on, of all times, New Year's Eve. Parrish did check it out; he interviewed with Mike Kelly on January 2 and started work the next day. The new century was one that bode well both for Lee and Jimmy Kelly's.

He says he loves working there: 1) because if he has a question or a problem he can "go straight to Mike and get an answer, right then. I may not always like the answer, but I don't have to wait or wonder," and 2) the contingent of fellow hardworking employees. "When everyone's doing their job, everything works better," he said.

The cast of both prominent, unusual, and engaging characters who make up Kelly's clientele also "keeps life interesting," according to Parrish. As so many guests have related, Parrish is around when "lots of high level (and occasionally low level) things" are under discussion at the bar. He says he counts on his natural "bartender's radar" to keep him abreast of which customer wants what and when, while also making every effort *not* to tune in to what is being said.

That radar has kept his pouring arm busy, lips sealed, his relationships tight, his friendships right, and the seats at the bar consistently filled. And the standing-room-only area in Kelly's bar is almost always full, too, because when customers find a bar they like, they really don't want to go anywhere else.

With his colleagues Robert and Arthur, Parrish—along with the rest of the restaurant crew—is an integral part of what makes Jimmy Kelly's so very . . . well . . . Jimmy Kelly's.

CLOSING THOUGHTS

A LIVING BRIDGE

It has been enthralling to observe how the procession of unrelated individuals interviewed for this book offered different yet similar assessments about Nashville's vaunted Jimmy Kelly's Steakhouse and why it has been so enduring. How does one summarize the magical "it" that has provided Jimmy Kelly's with such staying power? Like a giant sequoia, it seems to have evolved as a living, breathing, thriving bridge—a reminder of all that has passed and a harbinger of all that lies ahead.

A bridge, like a restaurant, is only an edifice until the people who built it and use it expend their energy in order to suffuse it into something sparkling with life. A bridge is a link and a gathering place that both transports and transforms as it joins the past with the present and points the way to the future.

People convene to celebrate, to console, to plan, to plot, to lead, to honor, to laugh, to cry, to remember, and to fulfill and be fulfilled, but, most importantly, to connect. Three generations of Kellys have created, lived for, and prospered within the city and with the people who have meant the most to them.

Cheers to them. May their future be bright with the possibilities of all that's yet to come.

Oh, and cheers to all of us too—the customers who live for the mellifluous sound of ice cubes clinking together as they land in our glasses, followed by a generous pour.

SOURCES

Associated Press, "Next Step for Oilers Move to Nashville Takes Place Tuesday," Deseret.com, November 20, 1995.

John McClain, "How the Oilers Left Houston and Set the Stage for the Texans," Chron.com, August 19, 2016.

Keel Hunt, *Crossing the Aisle: How Bipartisanship Brought Tennessee to the Twenty-first Century and Could Save America* (Nashville: Vanderbilt University Press, 2018).

Thomas George, "Pro Football; NFL Owners Approve Move to Nashville By the Oilers," *The New York Times*, May 1, 1996.

CELEBRITIES WHO HAVE DINED AT JIMMY KELLY'S STEAKHOUSE

Frank Sinatra
Dean Martin
Elvis Presley
Johnny Cash
Perry Como
Bob Hope
Hank Williams Sr.
Hank Williams Jr.
Mickey Mantle
Billy Martin
Roger Maris
Robert Redford
Mel Gibson
Dolly Parton
Reba McEntire
Sheryl Crow
Eric Church
Neil Young
Bob Seger
Alabama (band)
Lionel Richie
Herb Alpert
Eddie Arnold
Chet Atkins
Bill Monroe
Earl Scruggs
Hank Snow
Garth Brooks
Tim McGraw
Faith Hill
Dan Quayle
Mike Huckabee
Bill Clinton
Kix Brooks
Kid Rock
John Rich
Red Skelton
Ronnie Dunn
Keith Urban
Bryant Gumbel
Toby Keith
Al Gore
Jeff Foxworthy
Roy Blount
Jon Meacham
Lewis Grizzard
Julia Reed
Martha Stewart
Andy Williams
Larry the Cable Guy
Reese Witherspoon
Bob Dylan

Epilogue

NASHVILLE GROWS UP

Maybe its slightly shady past was one reason why Jimmy Kelly's remained a perennial favorite. Insiders still felt a certain cachet in knowing they could sit in the crowded basement with its red-checkered tablecloths and cedar posts—leaving the upstairs to tourists. And just about every famous person who came to Nashville, from artists, sports stars, and entertainers to politicians and tycoons, sooner or later made their way to Jimmy's place.

In many ways, the story of Jimmy Kelly's mirrors that of Music City.

The club's many regulars included Shelby Singleton, who produced the music of Jerry Lee Lewis, Charlie Rich, and Roger Miller, and the entrepreneur who purchased the renowned Sun Records in Memphis from Sam Phillips in 1969. Singleton also worked with Leroy Van Dyke on the 1961 hit "Walk On By," which *Billboard* magazine named the biggest country single of all time in 1994, and with Jeannie C. Riley on the 1968 #1 hit, "Harper Valley P.T.A."

In fact, the club was popular with the CMA folks. When Roy Rogers came to town to host the 1968 telecast of the Country Music

Association's CMA Awards, Tex Ritter introduced him to Jimmy Kelly's, and Roy and Dale Evans led their beloved horse, Trigger, right into the bar. The two stars were decked out in cowboy hats and boots, and Trigger wore his trademark silver bridle. To a fanfare of cheers and popping flashbulbs, they paraded the proud steed around the bar, then returned him to the comfort of his trailer before coming back in for refreshments.

Perry Como and Chet Atkins also came to the restaurant with Steve Sholes, a well-known record executive with RCA Victor. One afternoon, Sholes called my dad, Bill, at home to reserve their regular table. When my mom heard who had called, she started rushing around like an excited teenager. Dad took his nap, as usual, because he had to stay up so late at the restaurant. When he woke, he found Mom dressed for a party.

"Where are you going?" he asked.

"To the restaurant, of course. Perry Como insisted that I join him for dinner the next time that he was in Nashville."

"But what about the kids?" Dad asked.

She replied, "I take care of them three hundred sixty-five days a year. Tonight, you worry about them."

He took care of us, all right. He called my uncle and asked my cousin, Trisha, to come over and babysit for his three young hoodlums. My dad was a champ of a guy.

I've heard so many great stories about these years. Uncle Jimmy set up a Friday night poker game for his friends because, in the 1980s, many Catholics still observed meatless Fridays. At the stroke of midnight, the game would pause, as our waiters immediately began serving moist, tender filets and sirloin sandwiches so the players could break their fast.

Word of the game must have spread because one Friday night, thieves broke in with sawed-off shotguns. They threatened to kill

Jimmy if he didn't open the safe. They robbed the poker game, too, taking watches and rings—everything of value. What really shocked everyone, though, was to discover that the waiters and cooks had their own poker game going on in the kitchen with a much more impressive pot than the one Jimmy's friends had working at their table.

The thieves got away with hundreds of dollars and valuables worth many thousands, but not for long. Jimmy's friends on the police force chased the robbers on foot through the night. They eventually caught up with them in bottomland near the Cumberland River. Their message was loud and clear: don't rob Jimmy Kelly's.

I was still a teenager when Bob Dylan came into our restaurant for the first time. My dad had reached the ripe old age of thirty-six by then, and he was working the front door when Dylan approached with a group of music people—Charlie Daniels, Bob Montgomery, Bubba Fowler, and some others. Dylan was in town to record his album *Nashville Skyline* at Columbia Studios on Nashville's famous Music Row. I'd been hearing his songs on the radio for years, and when I saw him in our restaurant, I was thrilled.

Dad, however, had never heard of Bob Dylan. All he saw was a scrawny, long-haired kid in blue jeans, and in those days, male guests at Jimmy Kelly's wore suits and ties. "Sorry, kid," Dad said. "You can't wear jeans in here."

I was busing a table nearby, so I hurried over and whispered in Dad's ear, "That's Bob Dylan."

"Who the hell is Bob Dylan?" he whispered back.

I just rolled my eyes and said, "Dad, he's a legend, and he's with Mr. Montgomery. You've got to let him in."

So that night made history. Bob Dylan was the first person ever to wear blue jeans into Jimmy Kelly's.

One of our regular guests was Lem Motlow's son, Dan Evans Motlow. Everyone called him Hap. In 1956, Hap's family had sold Jack Daniel's to Brown-Forman, but the family continued to run its operations, and Hap worked in the Nashville sales office across the street from the Vanderbilt Law School. He was close friends with Bill Samuels, founder of Maker's Mark Kentucky Bourbon, and when Bill Jr. enrolled in Vandy Law School, Hap took the young man under his wing.

I've heard Bill Jr. say, "Hap was like a father to me." In fact, Bill Jr. has told me a lot about those years.

The two ate together at Jimmy Kelly's almost every Friday night while young Bill was in school. Following his graduation, Bill interviewed for legal jobs and received a very attractive offer from a firm in South Bend, Indiana. The first person he called with the news was Hap. Of course, they met at Jimmy Kelly's to talk things over. Bill told me later that Hap said point-blank, "Bill, you're going to have to call and tell them no."

The young man balked at first, but Hap persuaded him to try working with his father for just one year prior to taking the bar exam. He assured Bill that there would always be plenty of law firms seeking his services. Bill hesitated at first, lured by the prospect of a big salary and prestige. In the end, though, he took Hap's advice and tried the distillery business for a year. Ultimately, he stayed with Maker's Mark, took the reins after his father retired, and went on to transform Maker's Mark Kentucky Bourbon into a world-class brand.

Jimmy Kelly's continued to thrive for another fifteen years, although as Jimmy got older, my dad took on more responsibility. Eventually, the Harding Road lease expired, and by then, Nashville was changing again. Downtown had revived, and vibrant pocket neighborhoods were sprouting up everywhere. In 1982, my dad asked me to join him in choosing a new location.

These days, Belle Meade Boulevard may be considered Nashville's Millionaire Row, but a century ago, there was an earlier version of that grand street: it was on Louise Avenue, just off Elliston Place in Midtown. On that quiet street near Vanderbilt University, some of Nashville's wealthiest families built their mansions. Among them were Guilford Dudley Jr., president of Life & Casualty Insurance and US ambassador to Denmark under the Nixon and Ford administrations. His mother was Anne Dallas Dudley, the woman who'd been instrumental in Tennessee's ratification of the amendment giving women the right to vote. The Cheek family, heirs to the Maxwell House Coffee fortune, also lived on Louise Street, as did Jesse Wills, son of the founder of National Life & Accident Insurance, and who was himself chairman.

In 1982 the elegant, two-story Victorian home built in 1911 by Jesse Ely Wills became available to us. Dad and I knew at once that its magnificent rooms offered the same comfortable atmosphere that had worked so well for my grandfather John and uncle Jimmy. My father had the renovations designed by Sir Herbert Hughes, a San Francisco restaurant consultant. When complete, our new restaurant had four dining rooms and a bar upstairs, plus two dining rooms and another bar on the main floor.

Though Uncle Jimmy was retired, he came in often to provide advice, and of course we preserved all the family traditions—excellent steaks, buttery corn cakes, the Faucon salad, a loyal and attentive staff, and plenty of the finest liquor. Many afternoons, Jimmy would sit in our office reading the paper, and in the evenings, he enjoyed greeting old friends who came to dine.

He asked me once, "Did you know that every Tennessee governor since Henry Horton has visited one of our Kelly restaurants?"

Governors and politicians have continued to come. When House Speaker Ned McWherter was making his bid for governor, he held breakfast fundraisers at our steakhouse. He told me with a wink, "Most people won't order liquor at breakfast, so I'll have less cost." One night, he met with a group of influential politicians in one of our private rooms, then left them alone and came to sit with me while they decided whether to support him. I thought he seemed fairly confident, and sure enough, Ned became the forty-sixth governor of the Volunteer State later that year.

A friend of my father's once told me that "all the great things happened here" at Jimmy Kelly's. I can see his point. The decision to bring an NFL team to Nashville was made here, and so was the deal to construct the city's new downtown convention center. Movie stars and performers continue to find us too. Jimmy Kelly's has been described as "a Nashville shrine." We've earned our reputation as one of the grand old restaurants of the Southeast. I believe it's a fair and accurate assessment. Our ambience remains informal and clubby, with plenty of laughter and high spirits. As the late contractor Ray Bell once declared, "It's just a home place . . . where you know the waiters, and they certainly know you."

We've always endeavored to live up to John Kelly's original vision, treating guests as if we're welcoming them into our home for dinner and drinks. It's a rare thing for a family business to endure and prosper through four generations. Yet since great-grandfather James first carried his pot-still whiskey to market back in the 1850s, we Kellys have been satisfying Nashville's taste for fine libations. We've always made a point to do it with a genuine sparkling smile too. And our customers smile right back because they concur that we certainly do serve an exceedingly generous pour.

SOURCES

The following publications and websites have been invaluable in my research for this book, and I gratefully acknowledge their help:

"A Bootlegger's Story: How I Started," *The New Yorker*, September 25, 1926.

"A Judkins Bodied Packard Straight Eight Cabriolet Sedan," TheOldMotor.com, April 21, 2013.

"A Tour of Sites Connected to Nashville's Alcohol History (1865–1917)," Nashville Saloon History Tour, nashvillesaloons.weebly.com.

Adam Davidson, "The Financial Page: Real Numbers," *The New Yorker*, April 3, 2017.

AlphaHistory.com.

"Ambassador Bridge," Encyclopedia of Detroit, Detroit Historical Society.

"Commercial Aviation 1920 to 1930," Century-of-flight.net, October 22, 2019.

BelleMeadePlantation.com

Bill Cooke, "Sixty Years Before the Cocaine Cowboys, Miami Was the Wild West of Prohibition," *Miami New Times*, February 23, 2016.

"Bootleggers, Bandits and Badges," (series) *TIME*, 2016, http://content.time.com/time/specials/packages/completelist/0,29569,1864521,00.html.

"British Colonial Hotel: The Landmark With Nine Lives," Bahamasb2b.com, April 1, 2004.

Casey Piket, "Al Capone in Miami," Miami-History.com, August 17, 2015.

Cathedral of the Incarnation, CathedralNashville.org

Catholicity in Tennessee, edited by Rev. George J. Flanigen (Nashville: Ambrose Printing Co., 1937).

Charlene Blevins, "Castle Studios—Nashville, Tennessee," *Paste*, June 1, 2004.

Chicago Tribune: "Officials Probe Booze Deals in Gang Shooting," February 15, 1929.

"The Story Behind the St. Valentine's Day Massacre," by John H. Lyle, February 21, 1954.

Christopher Havern, "The Great Ohio, Mississippi River Valley Flood of 1937," United States Coast Guard, June 4, 2011.

CinemaTreasures.org.

"Club History," Richland Golf Course Maintenance, https://RichlandGCM.wordpress.com/club-history/.

"Coffin Ships: Death and Pestilence on the Atlantic," Irish-Genealogy-Toolkit.com.

Daniel Okrent, *Last Call, The Rise and Fall of Prohibition* (New York: Scribner, 2010).

David Stevenson, "Aftermath of World War One," British Library, January 29, 2014.

"Davidson County Liquor by the Drink Referendum Passes," *Nashville Post*, September 28, 1967.

Debie Oeser Cox, "Tennessee Theater and the Sudekum Building," NashvilleHistory.blogspot.com, June 17, 2013.

"Detroit During Prohibition: Bootlegger's Dream Town," *The Detroit News*, January 23, 2022.

Donald L. Canney, Rum War, The U.S. Coast Guard and Prohibition," (pamphlet) USCG.

Edward Behr, *Prohibition* (New York: Arcade Publishing, 2011).

"Eliot Ness," Biography.com.

Ellen NicKenzie Lawson, *Smugglers, Bootleggers, and Scofflaws: Prohibition and New York City* (Albany, NY: Excelsior Editions, 2013).

Encyclopedia Britannica (https://www.britannica.com).

"Florida in the 1920s," FloridaHistory.org.

"For the Love of Lager: The History of Anheuser-Busch," published by Anheuser-Busch, 2016.

Frederick F. Van de Water, *The Real McCoy* (Mystic, CT: Flat Hammock Press, 2006).

Gaylord Dold, *The Bahamas* (London: Rough Guides Ltd., 2003).

Geoffrey Kleinman, "The Story of Maker's Mark," DrinkSpirits.com, 2012.

Gertrude Lythgoe, *The Bahama Queen: The Autobiography of Gertrude "Cleo" Lythgoe* (Mystic, CT: Flat Hammock Press, 1964).

GreatWar.co.uk

Hew Strachan, *The First World War* (New York: Penguin Random House, 2003).

"History of Irish Whiskey," thepotstill.irish/irish-whiskey-the-history-of-irish-whiskey.

HistoryLearningSite.co.uk

History.com

Insider Louisville, Sara Havens, March 17, 2015..

"Ireland and the Thoroughbred," Bloodhorse.com, September 1, 2015.

"Irish Potato Famine," The History Place (historyplace.com).

Jason Cohen, "The Biggest Distillery You've Never Heard of Is in Lawrenceburg, Indiana," *Cincinnati Magazine*, August 2, 2016.

Jillian Frame, "Tennessee and the Great Depression: A Brief History," *What's Cooking in the Park*, August 27, 2014.

Larry Getlen, "Prohibition Was the Perfect Excuse for NYers to Run Wild," *New York Post*, November 23, 2013.

Mary Ellen Klas, "Florida's Long Bet," *Tampa Bay Times*, updated December 11, 2009.

Mason K. Christensen, "The Saloon in Nashville and the Coming of Prohibition in Tennessee," Middle Tennessee State University, August 21, 2013.

Nashville Banner: "Barbecue House Opened at 1500 Gallatin Road," Ross Fitzgerald, October 11, 1961.

"Popular 216 Club Closes Its Doors," by Red O'Donnell, January 2, 1968.

"Five Bandits Get $900 in Robbery at Dinner Club," Susan Thomas, October 10, 1977.

"'Why' is the Poser at Jimmy Kelly's," review by Homer Blitch, October 5, 1978.

"Jimmy Kelly's Acquires New Home, Old Service," Staff Writer, September 5, 1982.

"Jimmy Kelly Gets New Home, Opens Near Elliston Place," Staff Writer, September 13, 1982.

"Jimmy Kelly's 'Club' Another Nashville Institution," review by James H. Jesse, February 26, 1984.

"Club Atmosphere Keeps Diners Happy and Restaurateur Kelly Hard at Work," Mary Nance, January 27, 1994.

Nashville Downtown Partnership

Nashville.gov

Nashville History at Blogspot.com

"Nashville Past and Present," by Christine Kreyling, www.sitemason.com

Nashville Scene:

"Something 'Fishy' at Jimmy Kelly's," Staff Writer, January 28, 1987.

"One for the Road: Stories of Nashville's Hard-Drinking Nightlife," Ken Roberts Jr., June 13, 1996.

"The People vs. Jimmy Hoffa" (Parts 1 & 2), Jim Ridley, March 28 & April 4, 2002.

"Watauga," Bruce Dobie, May 9, 2002.

"Family Tradition: Local Restaurant Celebrates 70 Years as a Nashville Staple," Kay West, April 22, 2004.

"*Nashville Banner* Editor Eddie Jones, 1924–2009," Caleb Hannan, April 7, 2009.

"Nashville Businessman Nelson Andrews, 1927–2009," Caleb Hannan, June 15, 2009.

"A Nostalgic Stroll through the Good Old Bad Old Days of Printers Alley," Randy Fox, April 4, 2013.

"Jimmy Kelly's Retains the Charm of a Bygone Era," Steve Cavendish, April 30, 2015.

Neely Tucker, "Eliot Ness and Al Capone: The Men, the Myths and the Bad Man in the Dark," *The Washington Post*, February 18, 2014.

"Online Highways," U-S-history.com.

Peter Krass, *Blood & Whiskey: The Life and Times of Jack Daniel* (Hoboken, NJ: John Wiley & Sons, Inc., 2004).

Philip Scranton, "Revisiting Liquor Control in 1931," Bloomberg.com, November 28, 2011.

"Prohibition and Its Effects on Chicagoans and Organized Crime," University of Michigan.

"Prohibition Timeline in Tennessee," ParkridgeCommunity.files.wordpress.com.

"Racing in Ireland," Irish Thoroughbred Marketing, ITM.com.

Ray Hill, "The 1936 Campaign For Governor," *The Knoxville Focus*, July 24, 2016.

Ray Hill, "The Other Boss—Hilary Howse of Nashville," *The Knoxville Focus*, August 14, 2016.

Ridley Wills, *Belle Meade Country Club: The First 100 Years* (Hillsboro Press, 2001).

Ridley Wills, *Disastrous Deaths* (self publ., 2014).

Robert W. Chemy, "Graft and Oil: How Teapot Dome Became the Greatest Political Scandal of Its Time," History Now, Gilder Lehrman Institute of American History, January 24, 2014.

Rodney Kite-Powell, "Getting Booze Was a Breeze in Prohibition-Era Tampa," *Tampa Bay Times*, September 21, 2014.

Rutgers Global Tuberculosis Institute (website)

Sally J. Ling, *Run the Rum In* (Charleston, SC: History Press, 2007).

Sally J. Ling, Florida's Detective, SallyJLing.org

"Gertrude Lythgoe—Fascinating Women of Prohibition," June 28, 2011.

"Nassau—Wall Street of Illegal Booze," January 25, 2012.

"William 'Bill' McCoy—Notorious Rumrunner," January 25, 2012.

"Smuggling with the 'Real McCoy,'" DrinkingCup.net.

St. Louis Post-Dispatch:

"A Look Back: Jack Daniel's Distillery in St. Louis was Target of Crime during Prohibition," by Tim O'Neil, December 8, 2021.

"A Look Back: A Racist Defense Helps Jack Daniel's Nephew Beat a Murder Charge in 1924," by Tim O'Neil, December 4, 2021.

"Star of the Sea: A Post-Colonial/Postmodern Voyage into the Irish Famine," Alliance for Networking Visual Culture, University of Southern California, Scalar.USC.edu.

Tennessee Encyclopedia of History and Culture

"Tennessee in World War II: A Guide to Collections at the Tennessee State Library and Archives," Sos.tn.gov.

"The 1920s in History," https://www.1920-30.com.

The Brown-Forman Corporation, Brown-Forman.com.

The Catholic Church in Tennessee, by Thomas Stritch, The Catholic Center, Nashville, 1987.

The City Paper:

"City Spice: Mike Kelly, Owner of Jimmy Kelly's," July 17, 2007.

"Comparing Recent Events to Historic Nashville Floods," by E. Thomas Wood and J. R. Lind, May 9, 2010.

"Local Distillers Carry on Tennessee's Whiskey History," by Walker Duncan, March 12, 2012.

The Literary Digest, July 2, 1927.

"The Seagram Company Ltd. History," FundingUniverse.com.

"The Surprisingly Cool History of Ice," MetalFloss.com.

The Tennessean:

"Ike Johnson Fires Bullet into Brain at Southern Turf," February 4, 1916.

Book Review: "Inside Strobel," March 29, 1953.

"Fund-raiser H. E. Flippen 'Clearinghouse' for Metro," May 11, 1975.

"Mass Today for Popular Restaurateur Jimmy Kelly," Thayer Wine, April 9, 1997.

"History: Nashville Remembered Ryman and Fed the Hungry," David Ewing, December 23, 2014.

"Jimmy Kelly's Steakhouse Reopens after Renovations," October 2, 2015.

The Theology of Christian Resistance, edited by James B. Jordan and Gary North (Tyler, TX: Geneva Divinity School, 1983).

Tim Nash, "Organized Crime in the 1920's and Prohibition," TheFinerTimes.com, November 23, 2008.

Tony Gonzalez, "Curious Nashville: The City's Biggest Reservoir Once Flooded a Neighborhood, but Still Stands Today," Nashville Public Radio, August 25, 2016.

"Top Ten Prohibition Tales: The Untouchables," *TIME*, Time.com.

"U.S. Entered World War I," America's Library, Library of Congress.

"When Huey Came to Town," by David Ewing.

WhiteHouse.gov

Wikipedia.com

William A. Cook, *King of the Bootleggers: A Biography of George Remus* (Jefferson, NC: McFarland & Company, Inc., 2008).

William M. Leary Jr., "Woodrow Wilson, Irish Americans, and the Election of 1916," *Journal of American History* 54, no. 1 (June 1967): 57–72.

NOTES

1 Tony Gonzalez, "Curious Nashville: The City's Biggest Reservoir Once Flooded a Neighborhood, but Still Stands Today," WPLN News, August 25, 2016, https://wpln.org/post/curious-nashville-the-citys-biggest-reservoir-once-flooded-a-neighborhood-but-still-stands-today.

2 W. Calvin Dickinson, "Temperance," Tennessee Encyclopedia, March 2, 2018, https://tennesseeencyclopedia.net/entries/temperance.

3 Cooper v. State, 123 Tenn. 37 (1909), Caselaw Access Project, Harvard Law School, https://cite.case.law/tenn/123/37.

4 Cooper v. State.

5 W. Calvin Dickinson, "Temperance," Tennessee Encyclopedia, March 2, 2018, https://tennesseeencyclopedia.net/entries/temperance.

6 "Press Unanimous in Approval of Cooper Verdict," *The Tennessean*, March 22, 1909, https://www.proquest.com/hnpnashvilletennesseanshell/docview/904781206/BD27C06A5D674B6BPQ/2?accountid=33208.

7 "Ike Johnson Fires Bullet into Brain at Southern Turf," *The Tennessean*, February 4, 1916, https://www.newspapers.com/clip/38737257/191624-ike-johnson-fires-bullet-into-b.

8 "Ike Johnson Fires Bullet into Brain at Southern Turf."

9 "Cathedral History," Cathedral of the Incarnation, Cathedral of the Roman Catholic Diocese of Nashville, accessed May 17, 2022, https://cathedralnashville.org/history/cathedral-history/.

10 Jackie Finch, "Run for the Roses Begins at Belle Meade," *The Herald-Times*, April 18, 2004, https://www.heraldtimesonline.com/story/news/2004/04/18/run-for-the-roses-begins-at-belle-meade/48440073; Old Uncle Gib, "Pedigree of Derby Winners," *Crossville Chronicle*, May 13, 2014, https://www.crossville-chronicle.com/news/local_news/pedigree-of-derby-winners/article_9dbd72f6-10e1-5335-a8e0-58e718b40bda.html.

11 History.com Editors, "Teapot Dome Scandal," history.com, updated April 11, 2022, https://www.history.com/topics/roaring-twenties/teapot-dome-scandal; "BRIA 24 4 The Teapot Dome Scandal," Constitutional Rights Foundation, Bill of Rights in

Action 24, no. 4 (Spring 2009), https://www.crf-usa.org/bill-of-rights-in-action/bria-24-4-the-teapot-dome-scandal.html.

12 For more information about Bill McCoy, see Source section, specifically "Smuggling with the Real McCoy," DrinkingCup.net; The Real McCoy by Frederic F. Van de Water; and *Run the Rum In* by Sally J. Ling.

13 "Bronfman," Encyclopedia.com, accessed May 17, 2022, https://www.encyclopedia.com/religion/encyclopedias-almanacs-transcripts-and-maps/bronfman.

14 For more information about George Remus, see William A. Cook, *King of the Bootleggers: A Biography of George Remus* (Jefferson, NC: McFarland & Company, Inc., 2008).

15 "Our Story," Jimmy Kelly's Steakhouse, accessed May 17, 2022, https://jimmykellys.com/our-story.

16 Details about the St. Louis Milking Scheme found in this chapter were taken from family stories, as well as the website https://jimmykellys.com/our-story/ and *King of the Bootleggers: A Biography of George Remus* by William A. Cook (Jefferson, NC: McFarland & Company, Inc., 2008).

17 William A. Cook, *King of the Bootleggers: A Biography of George Remus* (Jefferson, NC: McFarland & Company, Inc., 2008), 26.

18 Daniel Okrent, *Last Call: The Rise and Fall of Prohibition* (Simon and Schuster, 2010), 303.

19 "Florida in the 1920's," FloridaHistory.org, accessed May 17, 2022, http://floridahistory.org/landboom.htm.

20 Mary Ellen Klas, "Gambling's Long History in Florida," *Tampa Bay Times*, November 24, 2009.

21 "The Great Flood of 1927," National Guard, accessed May 17, 2022, https://www.nationalguard.mil/Resources/Image-Gallery/Historical-Paintings/Heritage-Series/Great-Flood/.

22 "Alcohol as Medicine and Poison," Prohibition: An Interactive History, The Mob Museum, accessed May 17, 2022, https://prohibition.themobmuseum.org/the-history/the-prohibition-underworld/alcohol-as-medicine-and-poison/.

23 Stories in this chapter ("Jimmy Kelly's Move to Belle Meade") are drawn from personal conversations between the author and those involved.

24 Jim Ridley, "The People vs. Jimmy Hoffa (Part 1)," *Nashville Scene*, March 28, 2002, https://www.nashvillescene.com/news/the-people-vs-jimmy-hoffa-part-1/article_65964f13-d7b3-5848-96f8-21d733938c65.html.

25 E. Thomas Wood, "Nashville Now and Then: Quenching a Civic Thirst," *Nashville Post*, October 26, 2007, https://www.nashvillepost.com/business/education/nashville-now-and-then-quenching-a-civic-thirst/article_f80d3dd0-1d1d-5be1-a408-8dcfdd68de16.html.

26 Wood, "Nashville Now and Then."

27 Wood, "Nashville Now and Then."

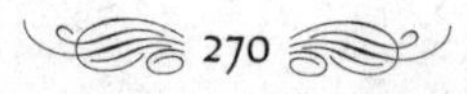

Writing this book was both the easiest and hardest thing I've ever done. It was easy in the sense that it compelled me to revisit and carefully examine the extraordinary history of all the Kellys who came before me, yet it was difficult because it's impossible to guess which parts of such a storied, but untold, legacy would be the ones that you, the reader, would find most captivating.

Nevertheless, this effort has taken much of a lifetime in its making. As anyone who's ever undertaken this process knows, it's far more arduous than it looks. There have been numerous longstanding, encouraging, and supportive friends who have remained by my side as I worked on moving the Kelly family storyline forward (and the fact that this book began on paper and concludes electronically accurately reflects the time frame involved in this endeavor).

Angie Smith, who has long been the glue that makes Jimmy Kelly's restaurant operate efficiently, was quite instrumental in the development of this book, as was Mary Buckner, who assisted me in taking a basket of old stories and translating them into paragraphs on a page. Chuck Creasey's creative talent shines brightly throughout this book, but one of his most significant contributions was his abiding belief in the project.

By wielding unrelenting encouragement, mentor Robert Davidson insisted that I write this book, which was as invaluable as the decades of astute financial advice and direction he has provided, while Bo Roberts's extensive epilogue, penned with his editor, Leigh Hendry, gave life to the personal experiences and recollections of a handful of special Jimmy Kelly's stalwarts.

Above all, it was the unwavering support, the adroit insight, and the incomparable friendship of my legendary brother-in-arms, Tom Ingram, that pushed *A Generous Pour* to fruition. As he's done with and for so many others, without Tom's insistence and formidable guidance, I might still be "thinking about it" instead of reveling in the accomplishment that comes with completion.

28 The dog Bell referenced was the police dog the Metro Police Department would bring in any time an alarm sounded at the restaurant. They had a standing agreement with Mike Kelly that any time his alarm went off, they would bring in the dog because Mike's building, with all of its dark nooks and crannies, was difficult to check, clear, and secure. When the alarm did ring occasionally, Mike Kelly would buy the officers breakfast while the dog searched the restaurant.

29 For current Nashvillians, in those days the restaurant was located where a BP convenience store and gas station now stand, right on Harding Road, adjacent to the Publix grocery store.